DERBY'S DAYS
The Rams' Rivalry with
Nottingham Forest

First published in Great Britain in 2012 by The Derby Books Publishing Company Limited, 3 The Parker Centre, Derby, DE21 4SZ.

ISBN 978-1-78091-007-9

Printed and bound by CPI Antony Rowe, Chippenham.

DERBY'S DAYS
The Rams' Rivalry with
Nottingham Forest

Gareth Davis   Phil Matthews

DB
PUBLISHING

Dedications

The authors would like to dedicate this book to their families for their continued support and backing during this project.

And, of course, to Derby County and its fans, without whom the great moments in this publication could not be shared and enjoyed.

CONTENTS

ACKNOWLEDGEMENTS

While researching and writing *Derby's Days*, the authors have consulted various individuals and sources with queries over match information, news, stories and more.

Thanks, therefore, go out to the Local Studies Library in Derby for access to their archives of the *Derby Telegraph*; the official websites of Derby County and Nottingham Forest and their archives of material; Mike Wilson and David Moore for their knowledge and information; the extensive programme collection of Gareth's father Richard; Gerald Mortimer and the various editions of his *Derby County: The Complete Record* book; the press departments at Derby County, Nottingham Forest and Burton Albion for their assistance in setting up interviews; the photographs supplied by Andy Clarke, Derby County's official photographer, and the *Derby Telegraph*; supporters who have reminded the authors of stories from years gone by; Steve, Laura and the team at DB Publishing for their guidance and work throughout the process, and too many websites to mention for those little nuggets of information to complete a chapter here and there.

INTRODUCTION

Ask any Derby County supporter what games they most look forward to each season and they will tell you that it is the ones against Nottingham Forest.

There really is nothing like a fixture against your local rivals to stir up the passion and get the football juices flowing by the time the day of the game comes around.

Any supporter will be able to tell you what they were doing the day Jeff Hendrick scored the winner as Derby triumphed at the City Ground with only 10 men, how loudly they cheered when Dean Saunders rose to head past Mark Crossley at the Baseball Ground, or how often they have listened to the iconic commentary of the 4–1 beating of the European champions.

As lifelong Rams fans we have experienced the great rivalry between the two clubs first-hand on numerous occasions in various capacities, and enjoyed plenty of good days but a fair few bad days too.

So with that in mind we sat down to write *Derby's Days* and not only celebrate the great and the good against Forest where the Rams are concerned, but also try and get to the bottom of just what makes the rivalry what it is and why it means so much to those involved.

We have taken a look back over the history of the rivalry to try and pinpoint when and why things became so heated between supporters of the two clubs.

Alongside that we have spoken to some of the people who have had an influence and an involvement in the major matches and events over the years with names like Nigel Clough, Paul Peschisolido, Alan Hinton and Roger Davies all giving us their thoughts.

And we have also gone into great detail on 20 of the Rams' most memorable matches against Nottingham Forest, looking at not only the game itself but the background and stories behind the encounter, post-match reaction and how it affected the season from then on, plus a look back at the career of a featured player who is intrinsically linked to the particular match.

Derby County v Nottingham Forest is a fixture that has been played in so many different guises but we have focused just on senior competitive matches since the inception of the Football League in 1888 and used the subsequent occasions and events as the basis for *Derby's Days*.

Lots of hours have gone in to *Derby's Days* but as Rams supporters there is no way that writing about Derby beating Forest on numerous occasions can be deemed 'work'. So we only hope that you enjoy reading this book as much as we enjoyed putting it all together!

Gareth Davis and Phil Matthews

HISTORY OF THE RIVALRY

Derby County v Nottingham Forest is classed in footballing circles as a 'local derby' – but before we look back at more than a century of rivalry between the two clubs, what makes a local derby in the first place?

There are a number of different definitions of the phrase local derby, each with varying levels of credence though with none appearing to be absolutely concrete in its accuracy.

One belief is that the idea of a local derby initially arose in Derbyshire, and particularly from the annual Shrovetide football match that has taken place in the town of Ashbourne since at least the 12th century.

The fact that the two teams of players were generally from the same town and competing against each other gave rise to the 'local' connection, although acceptance that this is indeed the source has been rejected by many on the basis that the term is 'local derby' rather than 'local Ashbourne', as it would be if Shrovetide football was where it began.

There was also a suggestion that the use of local derby emanated from the early days of Liverpool playing Everton, with their grounds separated by the city's Stanley Park – owned by the Earl of Derby. However, one of the earliest known usages of the phrase in this context came some years before Liverpool Football Club was formed.

One theory was not so much about the nature of the game, as the crowd in attendance and arises from the early part of the 20th century, when matches generally attracted fans of just the home club, with the idea of following your team across the country as an away fan was still some way off.

At that time, the country's best-attended sporting event was The Derby, the prestigious horse race at Epsom. However, when football matches took place between two teams based in the same town or city, fans of both clubs would turn up and with attendances increasing, the term 'local derby' was coined by the press.

That was in relation to the attendance rather than the match itself, though in time the term became more commonly used to describe the occasion instead.

But while no true definition has ever been proven, the most widely accepted version of events is also the most simple.

The Derby was founded in 1780, and records show that going back as far as 1840, maybe even further beyond that, the word 'derby' was used in the English language to denote a sporting contest and, therefore, a local derby was simply a match between two local teams.

In modern parlance a local derby does not just cover teams from the same city, and the phrase is used to denote a match between two teams that are not too far from each other – though the boundary of exactly where a game stops becoming 'local' is often stretched for extra effect.

The cities of Derby and Nottingham are geographically close, and just 17 miles separate the two stadiums, so the clash between the two sides certainly falls into the 'local derby' category.

And while footballing rivalries are far more intense in modern times than they were when the game was first developing in this country, the connection between Derby County and Nottingham Forest has always been noticeable.

In the 1880s both towns, as they were then, had two football clubs – Derby Junction and Derby County, with Nottingham having Forest and County, and although the two Nottingham clubs were older than their counterparts only Derby County were founder members of the Football League in 1888.

Forest, as founder members of the Football Alliance, did not join the League until 1892 and they had the upper hand over Derby in the early years when, in 1898, the first – and so far only – FA Cup Final meeting between the two sides.

Neither had appeared in a Final before and Derby were favourites to lift the Cup for the first time having done the double over their opponents in the First Division that season, including a 5–0 victory over Forest just five days before the big day, although Forest had finished higher in the table.

Derby also had the great Steve Bloomer in their side but it was another one of their legends, Archie Goodall, who delayed their arrival on to the Crystal Palace pitch – this was in the days well before Wembley – because he was outside trying to offload match tickets he had previously purchased!

Forest opened the scoring through Capes on 19 minutes, though Bloomer had Derby level on the half-hour but Capes then added a second before half-time.

Forest also lost a player to injury in the second half and had to finish the game with 10 men but, as Derby pushed for an equaliser and missed several good chances, the game's fourth goal went to the men in red as McPherson wrapped things up with four minutes to go.

Although, if you were to simply look at pictures of the winning team with the Cup from that year, you could be forgiven for thinking that Derby had collected the trophy instead.

Convention in those days was that the official photographs of the teams would be taken prior to the match, both pictured with and without the FA Cup, on the basis that it was too difficult to get the players together after matters had concluded.

The theory was that the photographer would then destroy the picture of the beaten team with the Cup, although there were occasions in the following years that saw the incorrect picture enter the public domain.

In this instance, the team photographed with the FA Cup and wearing white shirts was indeed the correct set of players. Forest's kit of dark red shirts and blue shorts was deemed unsuitable to be pictured because of the lack of contrast on a dark day.

Photographic equipment was not of a high standard in those days so it was far simpler for the Forest players to don the Derby County kit for their official team photograph!

Unfortunately, from a Rams perspective, it was the closest anyone in a Derby shirt got to the FA Cup as they lost their first Final, then their second – to Sheffield United – a year later as the apparent gypsy curse on the club appeared to be having an effect.

The first meeting between Derby and Nottingham Forest had taken place on 1 October 1892 at the Racecourse, the Rams' home at the time, though despite goals from Bloomer and Goodall it was the visitors who left victorious.

In fact, Derby did not taste victory against their opponents from Nottingham until the fifth attempt, in 1894, with overall superiority in terms of results ranging from one side to the other on a regular basis.

Following on from that first meeting the two teams came up against each other in every season until Forest's relegation from Division One of the Football League in 1906 then, when Derby went down the following year, Forest returned to the top-flight as champions.

That has tended to be the way with the rivalry throughout its history – one side enjoying a period of success while the other struggles, and that was certainly the case as, for the next 64 years, Derby and Forest only met 12 times in the Football League along with a handful of FA Cup encounters.

The two World Wars did not help matters either but from the second meeting of the 1925–26 season – when goals from John Hart and Lionel Murphy earned a 2–0 win over Forest at the Baseball Ground and a double over the Reds on the way to promotion from Division Two – the teams did not go up against each other in League competition until 1953.

Stuart McMillan, the man who had led Derby to their FA Cup triumph in 1946, had still been in charge as late as the week leading up to the visit to the City Ground on 7 November 1953 but a 4–2 defeat at home to Birmingham City cost him his job with the Rams struggling at the wrong end of the Division Two table, having been relegated from Division One the previous season.

In his place was Jack Barker, whose 353 games for the Rams had come between 1928 and 1939, though the first game he oversaw as manager was a defeat to the local rivals – also 4–2, with Hughie McLaren and Ray Wilkins on target.

Barker's Derby went down 2–1 at home to Forest in April that season but he was able to guide them to 18th in the Division Two table, though trouble was not too far away and in 1954–55 Forest again did the double over the Rams to condemn them to relegation.

The second game against Forest that season came at the start of April and was the second in a sequence of seven successive defeats that left Barker's side rooted to the bottom of the table before the campaign came to a close with Derby in Division Three North for the first time in their history.

Just to rub salt in the wounds, Forest's winning goal on that April occasion had been scored by McLaren, a former Baseball Ground favourite who became the first player to have scored for both sides against the other on derby day.

It is certainly fair to say though that the rivalry, if there was any in the truest sense of the word, was far from intense during that period.

Newspaper coverage of matches at that time made no real reference at all to the local nature of the fixture and the reports surrounding the April 1955 encounter were very positive in their verdict on Forest.

The *Derby Telegraph* devoted most of its front page on the day of the fixture to matters at the Baseball Ground that afternoon and went into great depth about Forest, even discussing their 'deep roots in football history'.

The newspaper revealed that the shin pad owed its existence to former Forest player Sam Widdowson, who registered the patent for the equipment in 1874, while four years later a referee's whistle was heard for the first time in a match against Sheffield Norfolk, 'another pioneer club, on the Forest's ground'.

It was also reported that: 'Forest have always worn red shirts throughout their history and it is amusing to recall that the club's original equipment included 12 red flannel caps!'

Although Derby returned to Division Two at the second attempt, by the time they were back there Forest had been promoted to Division One as champions so the two clubs had to wait until the 1969–70 campaign to meet again on the field.

Off the field, they had met a couple of years previously over the signing of Alan Hinton, the former England international winger who Forest had taken from Wolverhampton Wanderers in 1964.

Hinton had done well at Forest but he was no longer featuring in their plans. Brian Clough and Peter Taylor took over at the Baseball Ground in the summer of 1967, and by the September of that year they had paid a fee of £30,000 to add Hinton to their squad in what would prove to be a bit of inspired business and show that the winger could still be one of the country's top players.

In February 1969 came the signing of another former Forest favourite, striker Frank Wignall, although his arrival at the Baseball Ground came from Wolverhampton Wanderers, and both he and Hinton quickly became Derby favourites.

It was around this time that the rivalry really started to warm up, helped undoubtedly by the success of Wignall and Hinton, though on 29 November 1969 the first Division One meeting between the two sides since 1906 saw Forest silence the Baseball Ground with a 2–0 victory.

A Forest star at that time was classy Welsh wing-half Terry Hennessey, though by the time of the return meeting at the City Ground the following March Hennessey could be found in a Derby shirt.

It was a surprise to see the Reds let him go given his form there, particularly so to the team just up the road, while the signing of Hennessey was a true signal of intent for Derby as they splashed out £100,000 – breaking their transfer record and spending a six-figure sum on a player for the first time.

Hennessey was in the Derby side that won at the City Ground and that was to be the theme for the first two seasons back in Division One with the away side winning each respective fixture.

And there was yet more controversy on the transfer front as Derby went after Forest midfielder Henry Newton but, following on from the deals for Hinton and Hennessey, the Reds felt that enough was enough and refused to do business with the Rams.

Newton moved to Everton in October 1970 but Clough and Taylor eventually got their man, for £100,000 in September 1973, the last major signing before their acrimonious departure.

The 1971–72 campaign once again saw a case of 'boom' for one club and 'bust' for the other as Derby did the double over their rivals, winning 2–0 at the City Ground and 4–0 at the Baseball Ground on the way to their first League Championship, while Forest were relegated to Division Two.

And if that was not enough, March 1972 saw one of the most famous incidents between the two clubs that left Derby with a bit of egg on their face.

Eager to strengthen their squad for the title run-in, Clough and Taylor thought they had captured one-time England winger Ian Storey-Moore from Forest, and were so confident they had their man that he was paraded on the pitch at the Baseball Ground one matchday.

However, the transfer formalities had not been completed and Storey-Moore, rather than joining Derby's push for the Championship, ended up moving to Manchester United where he retired through injury in 1974, the same year the Red Devils were relegated to Division Two.

Clough and Taylor's controversial departure from Derby in 1973 meant the Rams needed a new manager quickly and, given his iconic playing career with the club, only one man could really fill the job – Dave Mackay.

The trouble was, Mackay was in employment as manager of Nottingham Forest. Mackay did eventually move to the Baseball Ground and steadied the ship before leading Derby to their second League Championship in 1975, though he was out of a job again before Forest returned to the First Division in 1977.

In charge of Forest by now was, of course, Brian Clough, alongside his trusted assistant manager Peter Taylor, and this really lit the torch of the rivalry because Clough had remained living in Derby and many felt that the club would have won more honours had he and Taylor remained in charge.

Just for good measure, the heartbeat of Forest's promotion-winning side was John McGovern and they also had in their ranks John O'Hare, two players who had been key men in the Rams' 1972 title-winning side before following Clough to Leeds United for his infamous 44 days in Yorkshire.

The first meeting of the 1977–78 campaign arrived on the second Saturday with Forest triumphing at the City Ground, and soon moving from Derby to Nottingham was Archie Gemmill – the Rams' 1975 Championship captain.

Gemmill played in that 1977 City Ground game for Derby and went to Forest a month later for £25,000 plus goalkeeper John Middleton, a disastrous deal for the Rams as it turned out.

Gemmill was back at the Baseball Ground the following January for a 0–0 draw, as were Clough and Taylor, but while it was evident that Derby's glory days were over Forest's were just beginning and they went on to win the First Division title for the first time in their history.

Forest then won the European Cup in 1979 and were European champions when they headed to the Baseball Ground in November that year only to be sent packing by Derby, now under the guidance of Colin Addison, who masterminded a remarkable 4–1 success for one of the most remarkable victories over the old enemy you will ever see.

As ever, unfortunately, the boom and bust cycle was continuing with Derby relegated to Division Two, while Forest retained the European Cup. Their captain on both occasions was McGovern while O'Hare made the last appearance of his professional career in the second Final.

Many Derby players of that era will tell you that had Clough and Taylor remained at the Baseball Ground, the Rams would have won the League more than once and would probably have become European champions too.

And while the rivalry was intensifying on the pitch, off it things were starting to turn nasty. Football hooliganism was starting to rear its ugly head with clubs like Leeds and Millwall having particular problems with their supporters.

There were several unsavoury incidents too between Derby and Forest fans, so in that sense it was perhaps a blessing in disguise that the Rams had been relegated.

The Clough/Taylor era at Forest came to an end in 1982 when Taylor retired but in August 1982 Taylor was back in football having returned to the Baseball Ground and taken over as Derby's manager.

It was an unexpected move and Taylor would get one up on his old boss in January 1983 in the third round of the FA Cup when Derby and Forest were drawn together at the Baseball Ground.

They were still separated by a division but a free-kick by Archie Gemmill, back for his second spell at Derby, and a goal for young Andy Hill, were enough to see Taylor's men to a thrilling 2–0 win.

In the summer of 1983 Derby signed winger John Robertson from Forest in what became a very controversial deal that contributed to the breakdown in the relationship between Clough and Taylor.

Taylor did not see the season out as Derby almost went out of business altogether, though they dropped into Division Three just nine years after becoming League champions. Ironically, the last time they had been relegated to the third tier came nine years after winning the FA Cup.

But Derby stabilised and turned things around, returning to Division One for 1987–88 only to lose their two meetings with Forest that season, and even in the following campaign they could only muster a point against the Reds.

That was despite Derby finishing fifth, their highest top-flight position since they came fourth under Dave Mackay in 1976. Just for good measure Forest finished third, six points further on, while also winning the League Cup and the Full Members Cup.

Forest continued to have the upper hand on the field whenever the two sides met, though in November 1990 came a rare bright moment for the Rams in a season that saw them tumble spectacularly out of Division One as Craig Ramage and Dean Saunders scored the goals that earned a 2–1 win at the Baseball Ground.

Forest's subsequent relegation in 1993 came from the Premier League, as Division One had become, and it also marked the end of an era with Brian Clough's retirement as manager.

One element to the rivalry among supporters has often been which of the two clubs was truly 'Clough's club'. Clough had a far longer spell in charge of Forest, including much more success, though it was his time in charge of Derby that first put him on the map and the man himself often said that his heart always remained at the Baseball Ground.

Forest bounced straight back to the Premier League as Division One champions, while Derby lost in the Play-off Final to Leicester, but the Rams eventually joined them at the top table two years later – meaning the meetings in 1996–97 were to be the first in the new era of English football.

Both were drawn, though the City Ground encounter had an interesting twist as Forest's scoring was opened by Dean Saunders – a Derby County legend netting against his old club inside a minute of appearing against them for the first time.

Forest were relegated that season but again went straight back up, and in 1998–99 the Sky Sports cameras were at the City Ground to capture a dramatic 2–2 draw that saw Derby's equaliser come from Horacio Carbonari, who then went on to further endear himself to Rams fans with a late winner in the return match at Pride Park Stadium the following April.

The customary roller coaster was continuing with Forest's second relegation from the Premier League in three seasons and it was not until Derby came down in 2002–03 that the teams met again, with Derby's 3–0 defeat at the City Ground in March 2003 their last game under the managerial reign of John Gregory.

George Burley took over from Gregory and when he left Pride Park in the summer of 2005, he had the enviable record of never having lost a match against Forest while manager of Derby County.

His two away fixtures had ended in draws, while the two home games produced memorable wins – 4–2 in March 2004, with the aid of a rogue coffee cup, and 3–0 in December that year after a fine display of football from Burley's side.

The latter of those two games cost Forest boss Joe Kinnear his job and the Reds were relegated from the Championship that season before eventually returning in 2008 by finishing runners-up in League One at the same time Derby were relegated from the Premier League.

And that is when it really got interesting. As if a controversial end to the November 2008 meeting at Pride Park was not dramatic enough, by the time the turn of the year came around both clubs had changed manager – Forest legend Nigel Clough taking over at Derby, while in charge at the City Ground was Billy Davies, who had led the Rams to promotion to the Premier League in 2007.

For added spice the two clubs met in January in the fourth round of the FA Cup and the tie went to a replay at the City Ground, a night which went down in history as one of Derby's finest by the Trent as they earned their first win away to Forest since the days of Brian Clough.

Nigel repeated the feat less than three weeks later for a second success at the City Ground in his first two months in charge, while the honours were shared in 2009–10 with both sides winning their home fixture in a season that saw Forest miss out in the Play-offs while Derby struggled in the bottom half of the table, although the two main stories from those games arrived with mass brawls involving players from both sides on each occasion.

Davies would haunt his old club once more with wins home and away in 2010–11, including a 5–2 scoreline at the City Ground that lent itself to being utilised for gloating purposes by the Forest faithful.

However, Derby got their revenge in September 2011 in remarkable style by recovering from the early dismissal of goalkeeper Frank Fielding and going a goal behind to win 2–1 in a game that also saw former Rams player and coach Steve McClaren in charge of Forest having taken over from the sacked Davies the previous summer – though he did not remain at the City Ground for much longer.

Derby went on to clinch a double over Forest by winning the return game at Pride Park Stadium in dramatic circumstances, meaning they had beaten their great rivals in the League twice in the same season for the first time since 1971–72 – with Nigel Clough matching the feat of his father.

Interestingly, that result also narrowed the gap in the overall record of wins that each club has achieved over the other with Derby moving to 33 in all competitions, just three adrift of Forest's 36.

The connections between the two clubs have not been without their amusing moments though, and one particular occurrence from 2006 stands out.

Former Derby favourite Ted McMinn was the beneficiary of a match between a Derby County Legends XI and a Glasgow Rangers Nine-in-a-Row XI – two of his old clubs – having had part of his leg amputated earlier in the year.

Turning out for the Derby side, along with great Rams names such as Roy McFarland and Igor Stimac, were Nigel Clough and Stuart Pearce – McMinn having had an ongoing rivalry with Pearce during their playing days.

Pearce captained the Derby side, scored for them, and for good measure ran towards the crowd in celebration while kissing the Derby badge on his shirt!

There has also been a sense of rivalry at times between the cities of Derby and Nottingham, although in those instances football has never been too far away.

One of the most controversial incidents came in 2004 when it was decided that, to improve international recognition, East Midlands Airport would be renamed Nottingham East Midlands Airport. This was despite part of the location being in Leicestershire, there already being a Nottingham Airport, and EMA being geographically closer to the centre of Derby than the centre of Nottingham.

This caused uproar in Derby, not least for lifelong Rams fan Steve Elliott, a Derby born and bred first-teamer at the time. The *Derby Telegraph* reported that Elliott and the organisers of his stag party were boycotting EMA over the change in name.

However, EMA heavily sponsored Derby County at the time and Elliott was given something of a dressing-down by the club for his actions.

In 2006, the airport's name was changed again, to East Midlands Airport: Nottingham, Leicester, Derby, though again those connected with the city of Derby were not too happy as Leicester is the furthest city away from the airport.

Elsewhere, as the first decade of the 21st century progressed, the Football Association announced that – having previously missed out on the 2006 World Cup – it would bid for the 2018 staging of the tournament.

As part of the bidding process, the FA needed to select its host cities and with the intention to have most regions of the country covered, the spot in the East Midlands was down to Derby, Nottingham and Leicester.

Nottingham's City Ground had hosted matches during the 1996 European Championships but was unsuitable for the World Cup so a new stadium was in the pipeline should England win the bid.

Over in Leicester, the Walkers Stadium had opened in 2003 but was short of the required 40,000 capacity to host World Cup matches, as was Derby's Pride Park Stadium, though plans were drawn up to temporarily increase the stadiums while Derby also had the edge in terms of location, transport infrastructure and overall facilities.

The Nottingham stadium was subject to constant wranglings between Forest, local councils, organisations and residents, and was beset by other problems – even down to the fact that an exact location had not been decided on.

However, despite all of that, the FA opted for Nottingham's bid to become the host city for the East Midlands and included it as one of the 12 cities in its final proposal to FIFA, though ultimately it came to nothing as Russia eventually won the right to host the 2018 tournament.

In 2008, the *Football Rivalries Report* – undertaken by the New Football Pools, owners of Littlewoods – investigated club rivalries and produced a league table based on a survey of fans looking at matters such as the two clubs' records against each other, regularity of meetings, transfers, fan reactions, media coverage and other snippets.

Derby County v Nottingham Forest came in at number 11, although the report itself focused mainly on the Brian Clough eras at both clubs as a reason behind the rivalry.

It's a rivalry with well over a century of history behind it – and here's to the next 100 years of the Rams v the Reds.

CLASSIC GAMES

Nottingham Forest 2 Derby County 4

28 November 1970

Background

It did not to take the Rams long to take the mantle of top dogs in the East Midlands after their promotion to the top flight under Brian Clough. In the first season back they finished 11 places and 15 points ahead of their rivals.

It was also noticeable that players were being enticed away from the City Ground to join Derby and not vice versa. Alan Hinton had moved from Forest to Derby in 1967, Frank Wignall arrived via a spell at Wolverhampton Wanderers, while Terry Hennessey was the first high-profile player to make the trip after Derby won promotion.

It served to rub in the disparity between the clubs that Clough and Taylor could make silk purses out of Forest cast-offs.

The Rams had experienced some disappointment at the end of their first season back in the top flight when financial irregularities saw the club barred from European competition despite a final position of fourth.

The let-down of losing out, combined with the possibility that they had overstretched themselves, meant that after a bright start with three wins in the first four games they hit a bad patch with just one win and seven defeats in the next 13 fixtures.

The sequence finally broke when Derby beat Blackpool 2–0 at the Baseball Ground. It proved to be just the lift that they needed with a trip to the City Ground coming up next. Forest, for their part, were past their best and it was starting to show.

Report

The Rams were forced into making two changes. Terry Hennessey came in for the injured Roy McFarland and Frank Wignall took over from Alan Hinton who had broken a bone in his right foot.

Forest were the first to show but Peter Hindley's shot from 30 yards out was more hopeful than anything else and went well wide of the visitors' goal.

It was then Derby's turn to mount an attack, which they did, down the left flank but an illegal charge on Forest 'keeper Jim Barron by Wignall ended the move, with the Derby striker being spoken to by the referee – famed official Jack Taylor.

The early stages of the game seemed to comprise mainly of an exchange of free-kicks. Hennessey upended Ian Storey-Moore with a heavy challenge, but the ensuing opportunity was wasted.

The Welsh wing-half then found himself on the receiving end of heavy treatment from Peter Cormack. Once again the free-kick was wasted and the ball went out for another goal-kick.

Forest would have taken the lead with a Hindley header from a corner but Ron Webster was on the line to prevent the danger and put the ball over for another flag-kick.

This time the Derby back line was breached. The corner was not cleared and Bob Chapman, up from centre-half for the set-piece, rammed the ball home from close range to give the home side a 1–0 lead with eight minutes gone.

The game was certainly all action and Derby nearly equalised when John O'Hare was blocked off in the area and Hector had a shot from the free-kick that followed but it was pushed out for a corner.

Wignall was close to making contact as the flag-kick came in but could not quite reach it.

The Rams were getting plenty of free-kicks and corners, but were unable to make them count until the 26th minute.

The move started with a long ball punted upfield to Wignall who headed the ball on for O'Hare. He got past Liam O'Kane but his goalbound shot bounced away from goal to Archie Gemmill who scored his first goal in Derby colours as a result.

Derby started to raise the tempo with a goal in the bank and twice went close before the home team, against the run of play, took the lead again. After sustained Rams pressure Forest broke away and a right wing cross was headed home by Storey-Moore.

Clough's men dominated much of the remainder of the half, but were lucky not to go in at the break further in arrears after a shot beat Les Green in the Derby goal only to bounce clear off the crossbar.

The second half, unsurprisingly, had as much passion as the opening 45 minutes. Derby were convinced that they had the ability and the power to get back into the contest.

Eleven minutes into the second half they were back on terms again. This time Gemmill turned from scorer to provider. He burst into the penalty area and cut the ball back from the byline to the far post where O'Hare converted to make it 2–2.

It was noticeable that with an experienced referee like Taylor the match remained fast and furious without ever getting out of hand.

The Rams took the lead four minutes after equalising. Gemmill started the move by feeding John McGovern. His centre was met by Hector, whose shot cannoned off the Forest 'keeper for Wignall to blast the ball into the net.

The game was all but over as a meaningful contest after 73 minutes. A free-kick was awarded after Wignall had been obstructed and the routine saw McGovern complete the scoring for the afternoon.

O'Hare flicked the ball to the midfield player and from the edge of the area he drove a left-footed shot home to make the score 4–2 to the Rams.

Derby looked certain to further increase their lead a few minutes later after a six-man move ended with Wignall's shot being deflected wide.

Forest then had a gilt-edged chance to get back into the contest when they were awarded a 77th-minute penalty after Cormack was brought to the ground in the box by a combination of Webster and Alan Durban. Storey-Moore stepped up to take the kick but fired wide.

Whether the Forest players thought they could get back into the game despite being outplayed is uncertain, however, Forest fans started to vote with their feet and the penalty miss signalled a mass exit by home supporters.

They made the right decision as after twice taking the lead their team were comprehensively beaten.

Forest: Barron, Hindley, Winfield, Chapman, O'Kane, Jackson, Lyons, Richardson, Cormack, Rees, Storey-Moore.

Sub: Collier

Derby: Green, Webster, Robson, Durban, Hennessey, Mackay, McGovern, Wignall, O'Hare, Hector, Gemmill.

Sub: Daniel

Referee: J. Taylor

Attendance: 30,539

Reaction

Derby's next home game after the win at Forest was the following Saturday against West Ham United, so Brian Clough used his manager's programme notes to look back on success at the City Ground.

Under a headline reading 'WE DESERVED TO WIN', Clough said: 'Victory is always sweet – in a "derby" match, with a bit of needle about, how much sweeter then.

'I don't think many people would disagree with me when I say that we deserved to beat Forest. They hit the crossbar in the first half, apart from scoring two goals, and Ian Moore later missed from the penalty spot having gone close with a fiercely-struck free-kick not long before...fair enough.

'But, brightly though Forest began, they would have been lucky to score either of those goals against a Derby County defence in top form.

'And when we pushed forward in the second half, we took complete control, and nobody played a bigger part in our success than Archie Gemmill.

'He's settling in now, and his teammates are getting to know what they can expect from him. The way he runs the ball at a defence, able to keep control in tight situations or let go a nicely-judged pass, Archie is going to cause a lot of trouble to a lot more teams.'

What Happened Next

This was the start of the golden era for the Rams and although they never attained the consistency during this particular season to challenge for any of the major domestic honours they did finish in a creditable ninth position while Forest continued their decline, ending up seven places below Derby in 16th.

The Rams had a potent attack and there were only four clubs in the division to hit more than Derby's final total of 56 goals.

John O'Hare headed their scoring charts with 13 in Division One and one each in the FA Cup and League Cup. Kevin Hector backed him up with 12 Division One goals and 13 overall while Alan Hinton also reached 12, with 10 coming in Division One.

Derby failed to back up their victory against Forest and went down 4–2 in their home match with West Ham, then failed to win another game until 16 January – by which time they had played out the remarkable 4–4 draw at home to Manchester United that cost goalkeeper Les Green his Rams career.

Five successive wins in January and February gave Clough's men a lift but inconsistency dogged them for the rest of the campaign and they lost the return at home to Forest in March – continuing the theme of winning away and losing at the Baseball Ground.

But five wins and two draws from their last eight games at least gave them some momentum towards the end of the campaign and set them up nicely for the following season.

Featured Player

Archie Gemmill was signed by the Rams for his midfield industry although he scored some important goals during his career – Scotland fans still talk of his strike against the Dutch in the World Cup Finals.

The one he scored on this day to open his account would have guaranteed him hero status, even if it had been a scruffy shot, which it was not.

Gemmill's arrival at the Baseball Ground had been a fortuitous accident. Part of Derby's metamorphosis into one of the big clubs in England had seen them bring in a young administrator named Stuart Webb from Preston North End.

He arrived to take on duties as club secretary, but mentioned the performances of a young player called Gemmill at Preston.

Gemmill was signed by Derby and went on to play a huge part in their greatest days. Although there were those, in his early time at the club, who suggested that he got his head down and ran in a manner that suggested if the main doors of the stand were left open he would be down the street and away without realising until it was too late, he went on to become a great midfield general.

He captained Derby in Roy McFarland's absence throughout the second Championship-winning campaign and even went on to captain Scotland half a dozen times while at the Baseball Ground.

Gemmill became one of Tommy Docherty's early departures from the club when he moved to Nottingham Forest in exchange for goalkeeper John Middleton.

It proved to be a great move for Gemmill who went on to win a third Championship medal with Forest and a League Cup as well.

But he was left out of the side that first won the European Cup for the Reds and later moved back to Derby as the first signing of Peter Taylor when he became Derby manager.

It is arguable that he was the main factor in the club's successful battle against relegation that season. Unfortunately, he could not repeat the trick the following year and Gemmill ended his Derby career with relegation to Division Three.

After his playing days ended he worked as overseas scout for Jim Smith in his time at Derby.

Gemmill's full playing career over both spells at Derby showed that he played 404 games in total with 33 goals scored. He was also capped 22 times for Scotland while at the club.

Nottingham Forest 0 Derby County 2

30 October 1971

Background

In the first few months of the 1971–72 season, nobody in Derby was seriously thinking about what the campaign might hold – or if they were, they were keeping it quiet.

Although it would not have been a surprise if thoughts had turned to a possible tilt at a first title given the form the Rams found themselves in as they headed to the City Ground for a first meeting of the season against Nottingham Forest.

Prior to this fixture Derby had played 14 games in the First Division and lost just one, a 1–0 defeat away to Manchester United on 16 October in their 13th outing.

They bounced back pretty well, however, by beating Arsenal 2–1 at the Baseball Ground the following week as they looked to keep themselves among the top-flight's elite.

The build-up to the match began a couple of days ahead of kick-off in the *Derby Telegraph* with manager Brian Clough revealing that defender Ron Webster would be fit for the trip to Nottingham, but adding that Terry Hennessey was still a doubt after picking up an injury playing for Wales in midweek.

All of this meant that 16-year-old Steve Powell, who had only made his First Division debut in that victory over Arsenal as a replacement for Webster, would be included in the squad to travel to the game.

And looking ahead to the match itself, Clough said: 'This is an awkward game for us. With no disrespect to Forest, I would prefer to be playing one of the top clubs.

'Local derbies have their particular problems. They defy normal predictions, preparations and form. There are added tensions and the players on both sides put in that bit more effort.

'Our supporters could help us by making this virtually a home match. I would be very happy to see 15,000 to 20,000 people from Derby at the game.'

Never short of a word or two, Clough had more to say in the following night's *Telegraph* as he confirmed that Powell would not just be in the squad, he would be starting the game.

The youth product had earlier made his debut in the Texaco Cup before getting 20 minutes under his belt against Arsenal and then playing for 90 minutes in a midweek friendly against Swindon Town, and Clough decided the time was right to throw him right in at the deep end.

'It is a big test for him but we would not pick him if we didn't think he was up to it,' the manager said.

Both clubs had confirmed their line-ups ahead of the match with Powell coming in to Derby's midfield while Alan Durban was the sole substitute, with Hennessey out altogether – although with chickenpox rather than the kick to the calf that had forced him off for Wales.

Clough confirmed that Hennessey would be banished from the squad to ensure that his illness could not spread, and also reiterated his desire to be playing against a team high up the table rather than one struggling.

He said: 'They play a different sort of football at the bottom of the First Division and it does not always suit our style.

'They [Forest] will obviously try very hard and make us work. It is impossible to go further than that.'

And while Derby's form had been good leading up to the match, Forest's had been very poor with the home side having recorded just two wins since the season kicked off, although one of those had come at Huddersfield Town in their previous match.

Their run of results included a 6–1 beating at Tottenham Hotspur with the signs already pointing to a campaign of struggle for the team from the City Ground.

Report

This was far from Derby's finest performance of what would prove to be a memorable season but they certainly got their just rewards to record a third successive victory on Forest territory.

Most of the Rams' good work was prompted via John McGovern, who was back to his best form after struggling in the previous away game at Manchester United.

Archie Gemmill also enjoyed a good afternoon, as did 16-year-old Steve Powell who started a First Division game for the first time.

A 2–0 away win might seem fairly comfortable but with the Rams 'nervy', as described by the *Derby Telegraph*, it could have been a different story had Forest taken advantage of their big opportunity on 12 minutes.

They were awarded a penalty when Colin Todd took down McKenzie but Ian Storey-Moore wasted the chance and his spot kick was saved comfortably by Colin Boulton.

And while both sides were looking shaky defensively, neither was able to make the most of the other's uncertainty during a first half that lacked any serious action, the penalty apart.

Even the King, Kevin Hector, was having an off day as he was sent clear on more than one occasion but failed to even test home goalkeeper Hulme.

Derby, meanwhile, had Todd and Roy McFarland not at their usual commanding best but Forest were not able to put the visitors under any real threat.

The breakthrough eventually came on 58 minutes when McGovern went on a weaving run, pulled back a delightful cross that Alan Hinton would have been proud of.

Hinton met it with a header that was handled by Forest's Chapman, seemingly over the line, but rather than give the goal, referee Smith pointed to the penalty spot instead.

That didn't bother Hinton, who stepped up and with a powerful swing of his right foot sent Hulme the wrong way to put Derby in front.

It was the spark for the Rams to step up their performance and they eventually made the game safe 11 minutes from time through an unlikely source.

Full-back John Robson had advanced down the left before cutting inside with the ball at his feet and unleashing an excellent low shot across the goal and beyond Hulme into the far corner.

It came shortly after Forest's Hindley had tried something similar at the other end but found Boulton in excellent form.

Boulton had otherwise enjoyed a fairly untroubled afternoon, though he did breathe a sigh of relief midway through the second period when Storey-Moore fired in a shot that hit the bar.

But outside of a few moments Forest rarely looked like scoring as Derby saw out the victory.

Forest: Hulme, O'Kane, Fraser, Chapman, Hindley, Richardson, Lyons, McKenzie, Buckley, Robertson, Storey-Moore.

Sub: McIntosh.

Derby: Boulton, Webster, Robson, Powell, McFarland, Todd, McGovern, Gemmill, O'Hare, Hector, Hinton.

Sub: Durban

Referee: D. Smith

Attendance: 37,170

Reaction

Despite seeing his side pick up a relatively straightforward win on the turf of their local rivals, a third successive victory at the City Ground, Derby boss Brian Clough was not overly thrilled.

Clough felt the Rams' third win in as many First Division matches, which left them second in the table after 15 games, was: 'A poor performance by my standards, and by the standards my team have set for me.'

Derby had not really stamped their superiority on their hosts and had Forest taken advantage of an early penalty the outcome could have been different.

But Clough also hoped that the Rams' display showed that they were capable of much better, despite how they had started the season, and felt it would send out a message to people across the country.

He said: 'Others must use their own judgement, not base it on what I say. Even some of the twopenny-ha'penny journalists who come to our games must have appreciated that we normally play better.

'How else do they think we have got to second in the League?'

Clough also admitted to some stern words at half-time with centre-backs Roy McFarland and Colin Todd for what he called 'some mucking about, strictly unnecessary' in relation to how they had performed in the opening 45 minutes.

While he was not entirely satisfied with the overall team display, the result at least did give Clough something to be happy about as he acknowledged that under any circumstances, a win on the road at your local rivals is never something to be unhappy about.

And as he concluded his post-match summing-up, the manager also made a reference to Leeds United, with whom a rivalry was really starting to grow.

He said: 'We did win two–nothing away from home in a 'derby' game and you can't do better than that except win 3–0.

'You don't suppose Leeds are brilliant every time they win away, or home for that matter, do you?'

What Happened Next

One thing noticeable about the Rams' form leading up to their visit to the City Ground was the amount of draws – seven to be precise, a high tally before October was out, though they had lost just the once.

And after earning a 2–0 victory on the turf of their local rivals they cut out the draws but were certainly inconsistent for the remainder of 1971.

A 3–0 home victory over Crystal Palace followed but then came a 2–1 defeat at Wolverhampton Wanderers that set the tone for the final two months of the year.

The win-loss sequence continued throughout November and December as Derby struggled to string results together on a consistent basis.

They ended the year with a 3–0 defeat at Leeds United, 11 days after beating Everton at the Baseball Ground, but the turn of the year marked a turn in their fortunes.

January was a month of four games unbeaten in the First Division, plus progress to the fourth round of the FA Cup, then round four became round five at the start of February as Notts County were beaten 6–0 in front of 39,450 supporters at the Baseball Ground.

In the same period, Forest's form continued largely as it had done with the Reds still struggling as they fought to get out of the First Division relegation battle.

They won just twice before the year was out, at home to West Bromwich Albion and Everton, but five further defeats ensured they would remain in trouble through to 1972.

An FA Cup giant-killing at the hands of Millwall was mixed in with four defeats from five in the First Division to start the year off and that run took them into the return fixture against Derby at the Baseball Ground.

And after the Rams made it through to the fifth round of the FA Cup with that victory over Notts County they suffered a League defeat at Arsenal but soon restored order in their next match – at home to Forest.

Disappointingly, however, after a third successive win at the City Ground, Derby would not taste victory there again until 2009 – though it would be very much a case of like father like son when it did come around.

Featured Player

The arrival of full-back John Robson from junior football in the North East in October 1967 was largely an unheralded one but it was another example of Peter Taylor's ability to spot a talented player.

Robson was only 17 and playing for Birtley Youth Club but he came to Derby and made four appearances in his debut campaign, even finding himself on the score sheet on the final day.

He had done enough to show he was worthy of a regular place in the team and in 1968–69 he was an ever-present as the Rams stormed their way to promotion and a return to the First Division.

It was quite a step up in a short space of time for Robson but he handled it superbly as he continued to command a place in the team in the top-flight.

Robson was not the most physical of full-backs but he was a more than committed player who never gave anything less than his best in every match.

He remained in the team over the next couple of years and in 1971–72 he missed just one match as Derby's journey to the top was completed when they won the title for the first time.

And it was during that campaign that Robson, who also became an England Under-23 international while at the Baseball Ground, produced the moment that he is perhaps most remembered for by Derby fans – his tremendous surge up the field and excellent finish in the win at the City Ground.

The arrival of David Nish for a British record transfer fee in August 1972 meant Robson's chances were limited, though he did feature in the European Cup until Nish was eligible for the latter stages.

Robson then joined Aston Villa for £90,000 which was then the Rams' record incoming fee, and having made 211 appearances for Derby he was part of the Villa side that won promotion in 1975 and the League Cup in 1975 and 1977.

Sadly he had to retire in 1978 because of multiple sclerosis and died in May 2004 at the age of 53, with a pre-season friendly between the two clubs later that year at Pride Park dedicated to his memory.

Derby County 4 Nottingham Forest 0

19 February 1972

Background

The football landscape was vastly different 40 years ago with more than just a couple of clubs capable of winning the title.

Indeed, in the six seasons leading up to the 1971–72 campaign, the country had seen six different champions – Liverpool, Manchester United, Manchester City, Leeds United, Everton and Arsenal.

And while these were big-city clubs, smaller clubs from more provincial towns were also able to find themselves in the mix and that is where Derby County came in.

By February 1972, in only their third season back in the First Division after winning promotion under Brian Clough in 1969, the Rams were in an excellent position and potentially in with a shout of winning the title for the first time in the club's history.

Although one of the founder members of the Football League, major honours had so far evaded Derby with only the FA Cup of 1946 sitting in their trophy cabinet.

But under Clough, Derby were in the hunt. Prior to welcoming Nottingham Forest to the Baseball Ground they had lost 2–0 at Arsenal but for most of the season they had been collecting wins to keep themselves up with the challengers at the top of the table.

Forest, meanwhile, appeared to be heading in the opposite direction. They had just lost four on the spin and were well and truly in the mire at the bottom end of the First Division.

'ARE FOREST ON WAY TO OBSCURITY?' asked the *Derby Telegraph* in an editorial piece printed a couple of days before the match.

The article reported that five years previously, Forest were on their way to an FA Cup semi-final and finishing second in the First Division, their highest-ever spot, while Derby were 'lurching towards' finishing 17th in the Second Division.

Questions were asked about the Reds' transfer dealings which had seen key players like Terry Hennessey and Alan Hinton move to Derby, while Henry Newton went to Everton with Forest's directors refusing to do any further business with the Rams.

It was observed that Forest were weak in defence and struggling to score goals, and pointed out that: 'Some of the players seem to have become resigned to the fact that they will be relegated.'

And while the football landscape was different back then, so was the social landscape with the country in the midst of a strike by its miners that was causing massive problems across the land.

The Government had imposed power restrictions on many industries during the problems, even affecting football to the extent that games could not be played in midweek because that would have meant using floodlights.

And Rams manager Clough, the self-confessed Socialist, announced his intention to picket with the miners on the day after the game and revealed that he had given them 100 tickets as a 'personal gift' for the following week's FA Cup tie at home to Arsenal.

Clough said: 'I think the miners are a deserving cause. They are entitled to special treatment because of the job they do. I see them as a group of people I can help personally. It would be the same whoever they were.

'A lot of people are suffering because of this strike, including me, including everyone who reads this, but I am sure that nobody is suffering more than the miners themselves.

'They are short of money and they might well find that they have no jobs to go back to. I do not think I will hinder a fair settlement to the dispute by doing this. Nothing and nobody can do that, not even the Prime Minister.'

Report

As headlines on a match report go, 'FEEBLE FOREST ROUTED' is about as good as it gets from the perspective of a Derby County fan.

The 4–0 scoreline was significant for the Rams in that it meant they had broken the recent cycle of winning at the City Ground and then losing to Forest in the reverse fixture in front of their own fans, as had been the case over the last couple of years.

Derby dominated the game from start to finish and had complete control of the midfield with John McGovern particularly impressing, while Archie Gemmill and Alan Durban were at their best too.

That left Alan Hinton free to weave his magic from the left and cause the majority of the damage to a Forest side that already looked well on its way to relegation.

Hinton opened the scoring on 34 minutes after Derby had put the visitors under almost constant pressure. Kevin Hector was the architect with a fine through ball that set the Rams' number 11 away and the former Forest man did the rest with a delicate chip beyond visiting 'keeper Jim Barron.

The only surprise was that it had taken Derby so long to carve out an advantage but four minutes later they doubled it as Forest's defence was split once more.

This time McGovern created it and John O'Hare, under pressure from two defenders, showed strength before adding composure as he finished the chance off.

A 2–0 lead became 3–0 just four minutes into the second period with O'Hare again involved as he was fouled on the edge of the Forest box.

Up stepped Hinton to deliver a superb free-kick that had almost become his trademark and although Barron got a touch, there was no stopping the winger adding his second of the game.

O'Hare and Hector then combined with Hinton for a chance to complete his hat-trick but it wasn't taken, though Derby did not have to wait too much longer before making it 4–0.

Hector picked up a loose clearance after it struck him and charged forward with Hinton in support but, as the Forest defence anticipated a pass, Hector kept going and fired in a firm low shot to the corner.

Hinton and Hector both struck the woodwork as Derby went in search of a fifth, while at the other end Colin Boulton was only called on once, and that was very late on when O'Neill had a chance but the Rams' stopper was off his line quickly to save.

'It was all too easy,' reported the *Derby Telegraph*. Not that anyone connected with the Rams was complaining.

Derby: Boulton, Webster, Robson, Durban, McFarland, Todd, McGovern, Gemmill, O'Hare, Hector, Hinton.

Sub: Hennessey

Forest: Barron, Gemmell, Winfield, Chapman, Hindley, Cottam, Lyons, O'Neill, Cormack, Richardson, Storey-Moore.

Sub: McIntosh

Referee: R. Matthewson

Attendance: 31,801

Reaction

Media coverage of the Baseball Ground beating of Forest was hindered somewhat by the power restrictions imposed by the Government on the back of the strikes by the country's miners.

Manager Brian Clough was, unusually for him, quiet in the days after the match and by the time he next spoke up Derby were preparing for an FA Cup tie at home to Arsenal.

Attentions were focused on that fixture in the next edition of *The Ram*, Derby's official newspaper publication which was very revolutionary for its time and gave readers a different insight into events at the club.

But rather than speaking about the visit of the Gunners, Clough instead chose the occasion to voice his opinion on Derby's chances of challenging for honours.

Up to that point the club had claimed just one major trophy, the 1946 FA Cup, and although they were third in the First Division at the time and with games in hand over the top two, Everton and Liverpool, Clough felt the future was less certain.

He said: 'I have no more miracles in my locker. What the Rams have achieved so far in recent seasons is nothing short of miraculous, but we have now reached a turning point.

'The age of the quarter-million-pound transfer has now arrived; it will probably happen before the end of the season…and Derby County simply cannot compete as things stand.

'We just haven't the money. Whenever a top player looks like coming available, we are often linked with him, together with Arsenal, Manchester United, Leeds United and the rest, as possible bidders.

'This is very flattering – but not realistic. We cannot find that kind of money in our present situation, and even if we could, we then could not pay the appropriate wages.'

Arsenal's Peter Storey was highlighted as an example as he was believed to be available but the England defender's wage demands would have been well out of Derby's range.

Clough continued: 'Peter Taylor and myself will continue to scour the country in the search for players to improve the team, but we can no longer pull signings such as Roy McFarland, John O'Hare and Alan Hinton out of the hat.

The Rams' Rivalry with Nottingham Forest

'Things have now reached the stage where even Colin Todd, at £170,000, was cheap at the price. We deserve credit for seeing this at the time but everyone else has woken up to the fact, and we will be outbid next time.

'Unfair in a way, of course, but money talks. Until, or rather unless, we begin to attract several thousand more spectators – and what more can we do to bring them in – we will have to make do as we are.'

What Happened Next

The result was certainly a boost for Derby as they went on to continue their good recent form in the weeks after beating Forest at the Baseball Ground.

Although their FA Cup hopes were ended by Arsenal at the third attempt, in the days of replays and second replays, Derby did not lose again in the First Division until 3 April when beaten at home by Newcastle United, their only defeat in front of their own fans all season.

In that time they struck what might have been a crucial blow in the title race by beating Leeds United 2–0 at the Baseball Ground.

The longer the season went on the more the feeling grew that perhaps Derby might just be able to really upset the apple-cart and become champions for the first time in their history.

It had been a decade since one of the 'smaller' clubs had managed to break through at the top, with Ipswich Town claiming the honours in their first season after winning promotion, and outside of Derby the feeling was that one of the more fancied outfits would prevail.

But inside the club, and within the town as it was then, the belief that the Rams were indeed capable of pulling off a shock was there.

A defeat at Manchester City in their penultimate game hindered Derby's hopes but their final match, at home to Liverpool, would go down in legend as the night John McGovern's goal earned a 1–0 win and put Clough's men in pole position.

It would never happen in the modern game but while Derby had finished their fixtures, both Liverpool and Leeds still had a game to play and both could still win the title.

Peter Taylor took the players away to an end-of-season trip to Majorca where, the following Monday, they listened intently as Liverpool drew 0–0 at Arsenal and Leeds lost 2–1 at Wolverhampton Wanderers.

Both results had gone Derby's way and one of the Football League's founding clubs had become champions for the first time – while Clough himself also followed the developments while on a family holiday in the Isles of Scilly.

As for Forest, they responded to the defeat by losing five of their next seven fixtures before having a bit of an upturn in April with three games unbeaten, though those five points were not enough to haul them out of trouble and eventually their relegation was confirmed.

The Reds finished four points from safety and went down second from bottom with only Huddersfield Town below them.

And following Clough's points regarding more fans coming through the gates, the FA Cup tie against Arsenal was attended by a season's high of 39,622 at the Baseball Ground.

More than 38,000 were present for each of the Easter home games against Leeds and Newcastle, while the season-ender against Liverpool saw 39,159 crammed in.

His prediction about a £250,000 transfer before the end of the season was a little out but the British record was extended to £225,000 in August 1972 – by Clough himself, when he signed defender David Nish for Derby.

Featured Player

If you are connected with Nottingham Forest and your side is taking a 4–0 beating at the hands of your local rivals, it is always going to be a galling experience.

And when the man who scored two goals for the rivals joined them from your own club, the taste in the mouth will be particularly bitter.

Alan Hinton is the man in question, one of the true greats in Derby County's history having joined the Rams from Forest in September 1967 for a mere £30,000.

Hinton had started his career at Wolverhampton Wanderers and played for England while with the Molineux club, then repeated the feat at Forest, but the Reds felt he had passed his best and allowed him to move to Derby.

Brian Clough and Peter Taylor felt Hinton would be a valuable asset to their squad and they were proved right as he became the creator-in-chief from the left, although he was comfortable with either foot, with Hinton's delivery from set-pieces and powerful shooting ability bringing plenty of goals and assists to the team.

Popular with the fans, who affectionately nicknamed him 'Gladys', Hinton stood out with his white boots – a rarity in the game in those days – along with his playing style, which saw him beat full-backs with ease and more often than not pick out his colleagues with a deadly cross.

Hinton also added goals as he reached double figures in his first three full seasons at the Baseball Ground, before notching 15 in the League in 1971–72 as Derby won the First Division title.

He was not 30 until the early part of the following season, making Forest's outlook on his effectiveness even more bewildering, and Hinton again reached double figures for goals under Clough and Taylor.

Under Dave Mackay he featured less, and made just 13 appearances as the title was won again in 1974–75, then ended his Derby career on a tragic note the following year after the death of his son Matthew.

Hinton was briefly player-manager at Borrowash Victoria before moving to America with Dallas Tornado and then Vancouver Whitecaps, where he set a North American Soccer League record for assists that beat even Pele and George Best.

Later a coach for Tulsa Roughnecks, Seattle Sounders, Vancouver Whitecaps, Tacoma Stars and the Sounders once again, Hinton has remained settled in America where he is a well-respected figure in the game.

He is a member of the Crossfire Premier Soccer Club Hall of Fame for his spell coaching the juniors there in the 1990s and became the local broadcast analyst for Seattle Sounders, now in the MLS.

The role is now filled by former Leicester City and Tottenham Hotspur goalkeeper Kasey Keller, who will be joined in 2012 by lead commentator Ross Fletcher – formerly BBC Radio Derby's matchday commentator on Rams matches.

Hinton's 83 goals in 316 appearances for Derby also saw him recognised in 2009 with a place in the All Time XI to mark the club's 125th anniversary.

Nottingham Forest 1 Derby County 1

26 December 1978

Background

As so many times both in the past and the future a meeting between the two local rivals separated by a few miles of the A52 served to highlight for fans the contrasting fortunes of the two clubs.

By this stage of the clubs' histories both had outspoken and controversial managers in Tommy Docherty and Brian Clough. Unfortunately for the Derby fans, both clubs were set on different courses.

Forest had finished the previous season as League champions and were set fair for another bash at the title, as well as the European Cup. Derby had been on the slide since the sacking of Dave Mackay and the board were attracted to the job done by Docherty at Manchester United.

The Doc, as he was known, burst in to Derby County like a hurricane. He knew that there were players at the club who had reached the end of their time at Derby but the speed and manner in which he moved them on angered many supporters.

He brought in a number of unknown and untested players in place of the likes of Archie Gemmill, Colin Todd, and Charlie George. New players came and went at such a speed there was little time for any of them to bed down into a team.

The first half of the season showed the problems that mass changes could cause. In the months leading up to this game they had lost more than they had won (10 defeats as opposed to seven wins) with the occasional draw thrown in.

It was hardly surprising that Rams fans making the short journey into Nottingham for the Boxing Day match travelled more in hope than expectation.

Report

Given the extra pedigree of the home side it was unsurprising that Forest dominated much of the game.

It was pretty much one way traffic with David McKellar given plenty of opportunities to show what he could do in the Rams' goal. Twice he had to leave his line and dive bravely at the feet of Tony Woodcock to prevent certain goals.

The feeling seemed to be that McKellar was setting out his stall to claim the goalkeeping jersey from John Middleton.

It was constant attacking from the team in red from the first minute, but despite all the pressure, Derby's defence refused to buckle. The experience of David Webb and Roy McFarland saw to that.

Playing conditions were not the best but McFarland managed to use his experience to adapt to them, as did John McGovern for Forest, who gave a masterclass in midfield play.

Although the Derby defence worked manfully to stem the tide of red shirts something had to give, and with 20 minutes on the clock the home side looked to have made the breakthrough their play deserved.

Archie Gemmill, as he had done so many times with Derby, bored his way into the opposition penalty area only to be bundled over by Webb.

John Robertson very rarely missed from the spot and spectators felt that his goal would provide the impetus for victory or defeat, depending on which colours you wore.

Incredibly the moment was wasted without McKellar even having to make a save. The usually infallible Robertson blasted his kick wide of the target and despite their overwhelming superiority Forest still found themselves with nothing to show for it.

The miss did little to dent Forest's confidence. Garry Birtles twice went close, once firing narrowly wide and then having a header tipped over the bar. Even centre-half David Needham hit the bar with a header.

Derby had their moments, but not many of them. Gordon Hill was not having one of his best days, while Billy Caskey seemed to be outnumbered every time he got the ball.

The one real bright spark was Steve Carter who showed himself to be ever eager for the cause. He certainly ran Frank Clarke ragged.

The experienced full-back had his heart in his mouth with a tackle that sent Carter to the ground with 34 minutes gone but the referee took the view that Carter was no longer in control of the ball at the time of the tackle and play was allowed to continue.

Clarke perhaps should have learnt his lesson. However, he proceeded to make the same mistake in first-half stoppage time. This time the referee saw things differently and pointed to the penalty spot.

Unlike Robertson earlier, Gerry Daly made no mistake with his spot kick, blasting it straight down the middle as Peter Shilton dived, assuming it to be heading for the corner of his net.

The award was made so deep into stoppage time that the two teams did not even have time to line-up to kick off.

Carter was injured during the challenge that gave the Rams the lead from the penalty spot and would be replaced for the second period by Vic Moreland.

Brian Clough and his team must have returned to the dressing room feeling totally aggrieved. They had dominated play but had come off the park a goal down.

It was clear from the first whistle of the second half that the home side were determined to readdress the balance.

The Rams were nonexistent as an attacking force for the first 20 minutes of the half. Forest attacked relentlessly and something clearly had to give. With 70 minutes on the clock it did.

Birtles, who had threatened the Derby defence with little reward, finally helped Forest back on to level terms. He worked his way to the byline and, despite McFarland challenging him and the ball on the verge of going out for a goal kick, he managed to get in a superb cross which provided Tony Woodcock with an unmissable opportunity to head home.

It was a rare moment when the two Forest forwards gelled as they had spent much of the game looking too similar in style.

The only question was whether the hosts could take the game on and earn the victory that their domination demanded. Robertson, however, faded as the game wore on and Martin O'Neill did not have one of his more positive games.

On the day, however, McFarland and Webb proved a powerful and unbreachable defence for Derby, and Clough's men had to make do with the single point.

McFarland had looked imperious on the day and David Langan also emerged with much credit.

Forest: Shilton, Anderson, Clarke, McGovern, Lloyd, Needham, O'Neill, Gemmill, Birtles, Woodcock, Robertson.

Sub: Bowyer

Derby: McKellar, Langan, Buckley, Daly, McFarland, Webb, Carter (Moreland HT), Powell, Caskey, Clark, Hill.

Referee: P. Willis

Attendance: 34,256

Reaction

Derby County's *Ram* newspaper was particularly pleased with the performance in drawing 1–1 at the City Ground, suggesting that it 'will almost certainly turn out to be the most important the Rams have won in many a long year and it came as a result of as perfect a defensive performance as any team in blue and white has achieved'.

And it quoted manager Tommy Docherty as saying: 'Had Steve Carter not been injured just before the break I think we might have broken Forest's long unbeaten run.

'His absence most certainly upset our balance. Vic Moreland came on on our right side but our attacking was completely upset.

'Yet, for all their attacking, Forest never really looked like winning it. I was proud of our lads, very proud indeed.'

The loss of Carter on a stretcher was a major talking point after the game, with the report in *Ram* adding that Forest 'were more than a bit naughty on occasions' while also addressing Forest as 'the "enemy" from Trentside'.

Later on in the same article, *Ram* also took the interesting approach of quoting an unnamed player in relation to Carter: 'If Steve can only get back quickly, and believe in himself away from home as he does at the Baseball Ground, we can win things more quickly than even the super optimists among us thought possible a week ago.'

What Happened Next

Contemporary match reports, though strong in their praise of Derby's defending on the day, were concerned at the lack of fire power, and Gerald Mortimer wrote in his analysis of the game: 'It is difficult, however, to see where goals are going to come from'.

It proved a prophetic statement as 15 out of the remaining 20 games of the League campaign saw the Rams manage to score one or less.

As a result the club finished immediately above the drop zone, although with six more points than Queen's Park Rangers below them.

Derby fans failed to warm to Tommy Docherty as manager and it was an irony of sorts that the relegation of QPR saw The Doc called back to Loftus Road for a second spell in charge as soon as the season was over.

It goes without saying that there were very few tears shed at his departure.

Featured Player

It was appropriate that journalists at this game picked out Roy McFarland as the star man, for the Liverpool native had been a class act throughout his entire Derby career.

He was initially picked up by Brian Clough and Peter Taylor after playing a handful of games for Tranmere Rovers, and was the pair's second signing for the Rams.

It is no secret that his preferred destination was Anfield, but when the management duo made it clear that they would stay at the youngster's house all night until he made a decision his father suggested that if they wanted him that bad he should consider a career at the Baseball Ground.

Clough actually told McFarland that if he signed for the Rams he would be an England player within the year, and although the timing was slightly out he went on to become the record holder for most caps while at Derby when he overtook Alan Durban to end his international career with 28 of them.

It was an England record for the club that lasted until Peter Shilton in the early 1990s.

McFarland played for the Rams throughout the Clough/Taylor era. He was an inspirational captain and considered by many to be the best footballing centre-half of his generation.

He formed an ideal playing partnership with Colin Todd and led the Rams to the League Championship in the 1971–72 season.

An Achilles tendon injury sustained while playing for England ruled him out of all but the final four matches of the second title campaign in 1974–75.

In the early days of his time at Derby he was nursed through the week often coming off the treatment table to play.

A combination of that and the tendon injury meant that the closing stages of his time with the Rams were blighted by injury. Without such problems he would have conceivably ended his Derby days as the holder of the all-time appearance record.

He left the club to become player-manager of Bradford City and saw them to promotion in his first season there.

McFarland quickly came back to the Baseball Ground as assistant to the newly returned Peter Taylor, but his departure from Bradford was mired with controversy and Derby were fined for making an illegal approach.

He stayed on in a caretaker capacity when Taylor left and remained as assistant to Arthur Cox as the club battled back to the top-flight from Division Three.

Cox eventually had to resign with back problems and this time McFarland took over as manager on a full-time basis, although he was not able to restore the glory days back to Derby this time. He almost guided the club to the Premier League at the end of his first season but the Rams were beaten at Wembley by Leicester City in the 1994 Play-off Final.

Despite his stewardship of the club as a manager not reaching the heights that he achieved as a player there is no doubt that Roy McFarland would feature in the all-time top five players list of any Derby supporter old enough to have seen him play.

His achievements with the club saw him recognised in 2009 with a place in the All Time XI, voted for by the fans as part of Derby's 125th anniversary celebrations.

McFarland, after leaving Derby a second time, was later manager at Bolton Wanderers and also bossed Cambridge United, Torquay United and Chesterfield, then took over at Burton Albion in January 2009 after Nigel Clough had been appointed at Derby.

His stay at the Pirelli Stadium lasted until the end the season, having guided Burton to the Football League for the first time in their history after Clough left the Brewers in a fantastic position.

Derby County 4 Nottingham Forest 1

24 November 1979

Background

The 1979–80 season had been a difficult one from the start for the Rams. It took them five games to register their first win and even though it was against high-flying Arsenal it failed to kick-start their campaign.

They had not managed to score in eight of the first 11 games, and as for the defence, some days they were on their game and on others nowhere to be seen.

In nine of the games before this match the defence conceded no more than a single goal. They did, however, twice let in three and twice conceded four.

By the time that Forest came to call at the Baseball Ground on 24 November the home side were clearly struggling. Five wins and two draws from 16 games confirmed that Colin Addison's men were in deep trouble.

Forest conversely had enjoyed a good start to their campaign, challenging as they were on three fronts, the League Cup, League Championship and European Cup.

November had started well for Brian Clough's men with victories over Ipswich in the League and Arges Pitesti in the European Cup.

Consecutive League defeats against Southampton at The Dell (4–1) and Brighton & Hove Albion at the City Ground (1–0) showed that they had hit a bit of a blip, but surely a trip down the A52 to take on struggling local rivals would get their campaign back on track?

Report

The Rams made three changes for this match. David Webb replaced Aiden McCaffrey, Gerry Daly was at last fit to play a full part after only featuring for 20 minutes since September, while Jonathan Clark took over from Gordon Hill who had been sold to Queen's Park Rangers.

Local derbies are, by their very nature, more difficult to predict than normal matches. The passions inflamed by local rivalries and the intensity of the play can act as a leveller.

With the two teams clearly heading on different courses, however, this match should have been easier to call than some.

Whatever the expectations of Brian Clough and Peter Taylor were regarding this fixture they were all blown away in a four-minute spell before the game was even 20 minutes old.

The visitors were largely architects of their own downfall, with the usually reliable Peter Shilton at fault for the first goal.

Shilton came out to make a regulation catch of a high cross from Steve Buckley. The England 'keeper failed to hold it and as a result only managed to present Gerry Daly with the opportunity to score.

Daly had been missing through injury for eight weeks and could not have wished for anything better than a gift in the 13th minute.

Shilton was again judged to be at fault two minutes later as this time he failed to deal adequately with a cross driven in from the right by David Langan.

There was real venom in the cross but a 'keeper of Shilton's pedigree would have expected to do better with it. His intention was to push the cross over the bar and out for a corner, but all he managed to do was set up a simpler header for John Duncan to nod home.

Mainly due to ill fortune with injuries Duncan's time at Derby had not been an outstanding success and his appearance against the local rivals came during his longest run of consecutive games of the campaign.

The next to benefit from the dodgy defending of the visitors was Steve Emery, who had been brought to the Baseball Ground by Colin Addison from Hereford.

This was not his first goal for the club, but certainly his first experience of a local derby match.

Having made the step up from such a small club he was entitled to assume that defending would be of a higher standard than that provided by Frank Gray who had an easy enough job to do in cutting out a through ball from Daly.

Gray failed to control it and Emery was on it like a flash, drawing Shilton off his line before firing home.

A half-time scoreline of 3–0 had Derby supporters ecstatic. While they were on cloud nine Clough was definitely not sharing their joy, and reports refer to him as stormy faced and very angry.

Rams fans knew that Clough would have things to say to his team during the interval, and having seen his effect on underperforming Derby sides of the past they knew that the Reds would come out with a different attitude, and so it proved.

It only took two minutes after the restart for the visitors to pull a goal back. Gary Mills, who had a spell at Derby on loan later in his career, was brought down by Daly as he rampaged into the box.

The referee did not need thinking time. A penalty it looked, and a penalty it was. Up stepped John Robertson, who had missed a spot kick the week before, but showed no sign of nerves as he coolly despatched the ball to make it 3–1.

Having pulled a goal back Forest were, though, unable to turn the game back around much as they tried and with 13 minutes remaining they were buried once and for all.

David Needham fouled Roger Davies and Buckley was again credited with an assist as his free-kick into the box was met by Duncan who got to the ball ahead of Shilton and guided his header wide of the England 'keeper to ensure that the match ended heavily in favour of the hosts.

Derby: McKellar, Langan, Buckley, Daly, Webb, Osgood, Emery, Powell, Duncan, Davies, Clark.

Sub: Emson

Forest: Shilton, Anderson, Gray, McGovern, Lloyd, Needham, O'Neill, Mills, Birtles, Francis, Robertson.

Sub: Bowyer

Referee: M. Peck

Attendance: 27,729

Reaction

Surprisingly, given the nature of the victory – a comprehensive thrashing of your local rivals who just so happen to be defending European champions – there was very little reaction in the days after the game.

But, not surprisingly under the circumstances, Derby County's official newspaper was not short of something to say on the success by the time its next edition came out.

Ram devoted an entire page to the win, including action pictures covering the goals and more, plus a little bit of a round-up of the occasion, although without any direct quotes from anyone involved in the game.

However, the newspaper reported: 'Well, yes, the most comprehensive and exciting Derby win in years was sparked off by defensive mistakes by the opposition.

'But considering the opposition were our fierce local rivals and neighbours Nottingham Forest the satisfaction was even more intense.

'This was a champagne day of champagne football that recalled the Derby County days of not too long ago.

'True, it needed Forest mistakes to get the adrenaline flowing, but after that it was all Derby except for a few minutes just after their early second half penalty goal cut the lead to 3–1.

'One great save from McKellar denied them, and Duncan put it safe at 4–1. Who will ever forget the exhilaration of three Derby first half goals in four minutes…few, if any of us!'

Not many people there that day will have ever forgotten the events of the game, which were so superbly captured by BBC Radio Derby commentator Graham Richards whose description of the game has gone down in legend.

His cries of 'Forest are in absolute ruins' will ring loud in the mind of any Rams fan who has heard his words, which can still be found on the internet at http://www.bbc.co.uk/derby/rams/2003/derby_forest_audio.shtml.

What Happened Next

Fans felt that, after the false dawn that had been victory over Arsenal, a win over their local rivals might finally give the campaign some impetus. If anything the win had quite the reverse effect.

Derby supporters did not see another victory, home or away, for another three months by which time relegation seemed all but assured. The sorry sequence saw 12 games played in the League and one in the FA Cup with a mere three points from three draws all they had to show for their efforts.

The worst of the matches saw them drawn away to Bristol City in the Cup, scoring twice while letting in six.

There was nothing to shout about in the return fixture at the City Ground as Derby went down 1–0, three games from the end of a season that saw them relegated in 21st place.

As for Forest, the inconsistencies of early season denied them a real shot at the title as they ended up 12 points behind the winners in the days of two points for a victory. They did, however, retain the European Cup and add the European Super Cup to their trophy cabinet.

Featured Player

John Duncan was born in Dundee in 1949 and having shown that he had an exceptional talent for putting the ball in the back of the net he quickly established himself with home town club Dundee.

He was so prolific a striker that he notched up 64 goals in 124 appearances before the big boys came looking for his services.

It was inevitable that Duncan would move to one of the glamour clubs south of the border with a record better than a goal every two games. So seven years after he joined them he left his home city to move to London where he signed for Tottenham Hotspur.

Duncan made 103 appearances for Spurs over a period of four years and he scored 53 times, an average of a goal less than every two games going.

In an era when referees were not so protective of forwards, injuries started to play a bigger part in his career at White Hart Lane until the North London club decided to let him go.

The Rams were keen to sign him and the forward moved north up the M1 to Derby for a two-year spell which was blighted by injury.

Tommy Docherty once memorably said after a lengthy spell on the sidelines by the player that apparently he had a bit of a history of injury.

Duncan may not have managed many games in two years at the Baseball Ground with 36 appearances in all but he still managed a respectable return of 12 goals.

He made his debut for the Rams in a home win over West Bromwich Albion on 16 September 1978 and scored what would prove to be the decisive goal in a 3–2 victory.

Duncan then scored his second goal in a Derby shirt in his third game and ironically it came against his previous club Spurs in a 2–2 draw at the Baseball Ground. He had already missed several matches through injury by this stage.

It set a pattern for his season – play a few games then miss a few. As if to prove the point he debuted in the sixth League game of the campaign but only featured in 15 more in the entire season scoring five times.

His second season with the Rams was pretty much the same, he played 16 times and this time scored seven goals

None would prove to be more memorable than the brace he scored on this day as Brian Clough's star studded team were humbled. It was a return to the Duncan of old as he took up positions that many would not think of and scored two good goals.

When Duncan moved on he played briefly for his final club Scunthorpe United where he played nine games without scoring, leaving him with a career total of 269 games played and 129 goals scored. He also played one game for a Scottish League XI where he scored twice.

After he called time on his playing career he enjoyed a successful career in management where he was best known for his two spells with Chesterfield that included two promotions and the remarkable run to the semi-final of the FA Cup in 1997.

Derby County 2 Nottingham Forest 0

8 January 1983

Background

There can be no doubts in the minds of either Derby or Forest supporters that the management pairing of Brian Clough and Peter Taylor was the best in the history of either club.

Clough and Taylor had built a Derby County side that was among the best in Europe, let alone England. Their achievements at the Baseball Ground are the stuff of legend.

But even taking the team to promotion, going on to win the top division title, and reaching the semi-final of the European Cup, only to seemingly be cheated out of a place in the final itself, paled slightly when compared to what they did down the road in winning the top division the season after gaining promotion, and following that up with not one but two European Cups.

As a pair they were supreme, but over the years cracks began to develop in the partnership and Taylor eventually decided to retire from football altogether.

Citing reasons for packing in that Clough was sympathetic to, the two men would probably have remained friends until the end.

When Taylor came out of retirement to help an ailing Derby his one-time comrade could see this as little other than a betrayal.

Taylor took over at the Baseball Ground in November 1982, and if his arrival was not exactly seen as the Second Coming there was much hope that he could reverse the downward spiral that the Rams found themselves in.

His impact was not instantaneous but his arrival provided a stabilising influence at the club. One of Taylor's first acts was to bring 35-year-old Archie Gemmill back to the club where he made his name. What a master-stroke it proved to be.

The team was not as high up the table as anyone hoped and envious eyes were cast over the county boundary to the old enemy who were sitting pretty in 4th place in Division One.

So many supporters must have wished to get a chance to humble the foe who were currently top dog in the area.

The fans got their fondest desire granted when the two clubs were pulled out of the red velvet bag to face each other on third round day.

Report

There were a number of connections between the two clubs going into the game besides the managers.

Archie Gemmill had played for both teams, while Gary Mills was on loan at Derby because a quirk in the ruling that allowed players to go on loan to North American sides could not return to play for their parent club during the American close season.

Mills also played for Leicester City and Notts County – making him one of a rare breed to have featured for all four major East Midlands clubs.

One surprise in the Forest starting line-up was the absence of Colin Todd. Bryn Gunn and Willie Young, therefore, formed the central defensive partnership entrusted with the task of keeping the Rams attack quiet.

That should have been a reasonably easy job given that Bobby Davison was unavailable and David Swindlehurst had been pressed into action in midfield.

The two central strikers on the day were Kevin Wilson and Andy Hill, the young Ilkeston-born forward who was often used in different positions too.

Despite Forest – as with all Brian Clough teams – having a reputation for solidity in defence, they found themselves increasingly bothered by the pace and tenacity of both Wilson and Mills.

Derby could easily have been two goals up before the 20th minute had Hill been able to show more composure and awareness in front of the visitors' goal.

The Rams were nearly made to pay for their lack of finishing when Mark Proctor came close to giving the away team the lead. A deep cross from Ian Walsh was met by Proctor who would have converted the chance but for the reflexes of Derby 'keeper Steve Cherry.

Mills was clearly keen to prove a point and almost scored direct from a corner kick. Steve Sutton in the Forest goal missed the in swinger and it was left to Steve Hodge to head the ball from off the line.

As so often this game was a tense and tight affair with no quarter asked or given. Even in an age when there was still a magic to the FA Cup it was a combination of local rivalries between the two clubs and the extra fact that Clough and Taylor were leading the two sides that gave the match its real potency.

The score was 0–0 at half-time but there was a feeling that something would have to give before long.

The breakthrough nearly came after 57 minutes. John Barton, raiding down the wing from his right-back position, fired in a cross that was met by the boot of Wilson. The shot, unfortunately, hit the foot of the post and bounced away to safety.

Wilson was, however, responsible for Derby eventually opening the scoring. The skill of the youngster signed from non-League Banbury proved too much for Young who launched a despairing tackle that gave referee George Courtney little option than to award a free-kick.

If Young was relieved to have timed the tackle so as to avoid giving away a penalty he would not have been happy with what happened next.

The ball was placed just outside the penalty area D in an almost dead central position. Swindlehurst ran over the ball throwing confusion into the Forest wall while Gemmill curled a left-footed kick round the wall and wide of the despairing dive of Sutton.

With 62 minutes gone the home side were a goal to the good against their top division neighbours.

Despite the supposed extra pedigree of the team in red the goal seemed to totally knock the stuffing out of them and the rest of the game seemed to pass by without a meaningful attack on the Derby goal for Cherry to have to deal with.

It is always harder for a goalkeeper in a game where he has little to do for long spells. The top ones can be kept idle for lengthy periods, but by keeping up their concentration make vital saves that hugely affect the outcome of the game.

So it was with Cherry on this occasion. The Derby 'keeper was so much a spectator that he could almost have written the match report from his goalline.

He was ready, however, when Forest launched one last sortie on the home goal. Gunn fired in a long range shot that Cherry had to dive full length to save.

That may have been it as far as the visitors were concerned but the Rams had one more surprise to spring.

With the game heading towards stoppage time the experienced Ian Bowyer was caught dallying in possession.

Bowyer was stripped of the ball and, with all the Forest team with the exception of the 'keeper pressing for the equaliser, Mick Brolly found himself with plenty of time and space to roll the ball into the path of Hill who carried the ball on before slamming home goal number two.

Derby: Cherry, Barton, Attley, Gemmill (Dalziel 71), Foster, McAlle, Brolly, Wilson, Hill, Swindlehurst, Mills.

Forest: Sutton, Swain, Bowyer, Gunn, Young, Walsh, Proctor, Wallace, Birtles, Hodge, Robertson (Davenport 70).

Referee: G. Courtney

Attendance: 28,494

Reaction

Surprisingly given the circumstances, there was very little reaction from this game to be found in the following days – but the next edition of the club's official newspaper produced the goods with some interesting stories.

Derby were not in home action again until two weeks later, when *Ram* next hit the streets, and it did not carry any direct quotes from players or management.

Although an editorial piece looking back on the game bemoaned Derby's recent inconsistency and said: 'Rams really are a conundrum, aren't they? They outplayed Forest in almost all departments, and knocked them out of the FA Cup here a fortnight ago.

'No fluke this, but it DOES happen in the Cup, to reply to Forest fans who couldn't believe what they saw.

'As Derby had also played as gracefully against QPR five days before, Rams fans thought we were on our way.

'Then came last Saturday's flop at Carlisle, to complicate the League issue. Will the real Rams please stand up today!'

But the most interesting story came in the shape of an interview with Uttoxeter clairvoyant Doreen Shadbolt, who had told BBC Radio Derby ahead of the Forest game that the Rams would beat their rivals.

And Doreen was also forecasting plenty of success for Derby in 1983 but only under a certain set of circumstances.

'I know nothing at all about football,' she said in an interview with Notty Hornblower, the women's correspondent in *Ram*.

'But I do know about God, and the spirits. If there is a player on the team especially, or someone in the management or the administration who prays, then so much good will result.

'Don't worry about the present. If one or two Derby players really started to believe in themselves things would begin to happen.

'They could start by saying a little prayer to themselves, not in public, before they go on the pitch. Indeed the more players who do that, and the more fans too, the easier it will be.

'More things are wrought by prayer than this world dreams of. Yes, people will scoff, but I trust they won't be Derby County folk.

'That could do more harm than the good I am earnestly trying to invoke. Unbelievers could darken the light which is now beginning to shine over Derby County Football Club.'

What Happened Next

Although the Rams lost the next game 3–0 away to Carlisle United, the belief that the side had shown in defeating top division opponents quickly manifested itself.

In the Cup they were drawn at home to Chelsea who they beat 2–1 at the Baseball Ground before losing by the narrowest of margins at home to Manchester United with the 1–0 defeat seen as a sign that things were improving.

More importantly League form picked up and an unbeaten run of 15 games saw them pull away from the danger zone and end the campaign in a comfortable 13th position, five points above the drop zone.

The final table showed that they had drawn 19 of their 42 matches. If they had managed to convert half a dozen of those draws into wins, by scoring six more goals the club would have finished seventh in the division.

Unsurprisingly, with the return of Taylor, the long unbeaten run and the thought of converting a few of those draws into wins gave supporters real hopes that the good times were on their way back.

Unfortunately, football has a habit of turning round and biting you when you least expect it, and the following season represented one of the darkest days in club history as losing an FA Cup quarter-final to lower division opposition and relegation to the third tier all seemed small problems in comparison to the very real possibility of the club going out of existence altogether.

Featured Player

The amazing thing about local derby matches is that you may not have the greatest of careers but pop up in the right place at the right time and your name can go down in legend.

Thus it was with Andrew Robert Hill, born in Ilkeston on 10 November 1960. Hill started his footballing career playing for non league side Kimberley Town before being spotted by the scouts and brought to the Baseball Ground.

The Rams' problem was that having seen his potential and given him games in the reserves to find his feet nobody really knew what to do with him.

A look at his playing record in Derby colours shows that he appeared in a number of different shirts and positions in a short career.

His first senior game was away to Leyton Orient on 16 January 1982 where he scored on his debut while wearing the number nine shirt.

He played six games in all during that campaign with his only other goal coming in an away fixture against Rotherham United at Millmoor.

The following season he was in and out of the team as he struggled to establish himself. He got called into the team for 12 League matches without scoring.

Hill's goalscoring exploits were reserved for the cup competitions. He played three times in each of the FA and League Cups.

His sole League Cup strike came in the home leg of the tie against Hartlepool United but it was the goal against Forest for which he will forever be remembered.

Hill managed just one game the following season – an away defeat at Brighton and Hove Albion in which he failed to score, before being deemed surplus to requirements.

He moved on to Carlisle United where he played a total of 85 times, scoring 15 goals before injury brought a premature end to his career, and he later became an accountant.

His Derby record read 25 starts, three appearances off the bench, and four goals scored. It is for just one of those four that he will forever be remembered by Derby fans.

Derby County 2 Nottingham Forest 1

24 November 1990

Background

It is fair to say the progress that Derby County had made in the latter part of the 1980s under Arthur Cox was unravelling by the time this fixture came about.

Derby had been in the doldrums when Cox took over but he inspired the club to promotion from the old Division Three in 1986, before leading the side to an emphatic season as Division Two champions a year later to lift the Rams from the third tier to the top-flight in successive years.

In 1988–89 they had finished fifth in Division One, their highest position since Dave Mackay's side came fourth in 1976, and would have earned a UEFA Cup spot had it not been for the ban on English clubs in Europe following the Heysel disaster.

That same season Forest finished third, showing that even when the Rams were doing well the Reds still had something of an Indian sign over Derby!

But Derby had been unable to kick on and were in a bit of danger of relegation in 1989–90, though they managed to avoid any serious trouble amid off-field problems and uncertainty under the chairmanship of Robert Maxwell.

By the time this fixture arose Maxwell was intent on selling the club and had recently been under investigation from the Football League over a loan to Tottenham Hotspur which went through companies owned by him and Spurs chairman Irving Scholar, though the conclusion was he had done no wrong.

Maxwell was seeking an apology from the League's management committee and at a sports writers' lunch had been asked whether Derby supporters might be angry if he had lent money to Spurs.

The *Derby Telegraph* quoted him as responding: 'If such a supporter exists, I would tell him to get stuffed. What right would he have to tell me what to do with my money?

'I could make Tottenham, Derby and Oxford suffer if the mismanagement committee do nothing.'

The *Telegraph*'s own editorial added: 'It is scandalous that a threat against Derby County, from somebody who remains chairman of the club, should be used as part of an attempt to force an apology from the League.'

On the football side of things, Cox was focused on ending Derby's poor recent record against Forest with no wins having been recorded against the old enemy since the two sides had been back in the same division.

The manager admitted: 'Since we came back to the First Division we have had six tries to beat Nottingham Forest and have not managed it once. That is not a record we are proud of and we would like to do something about it.

'There is always a crackle about a local derby and there have been some good matches at the Baseball Ground in the last two months. We are looking forward to it.'

Derby actually approached the game in decent form despite a terrible start to the season that had seen them fail to win any fixture until 10 October, when they beat Carlisle United 1–0 in a League Cup tie at the Baseball Ground.

That was the first of a six-game unbeaten run that also took in a 0–0 draw with Manchester United and a 6–0 victory over Sunderland, with only a 3–0 defeat at Leeds United ending it the week before the Forest game.

The pre-match football talk surrounded Derby skipper Mark Wright going up against Forest's Des Walker, the pair having played together successfully for England under Bobby Robson during the run to the semi-final of the previous summer's World Cup in Italy.

Derby also added young defenders Steve Round and Jason Kavanagh to their squad with injury concerns over Steve Cross, Mel Sage and Paul Williams.

Report

Derby certainly had to show all of their battling qualities to recover the points from this match having found themselves in a familiar position with just 15 minutes on the clock.

They were behind, which was a far from rare situation in the season and also against Forest, who they had failed to beat since returning to the First Division in 1987.

The goal itself was one they would certainly have been disappointed with as they failed to get the ball properly clear when they had the opportunity.

Steve Chettle's low shot had struck a post and was scrambled away for a corner, which the Rams did not deal with and the ball was touched back for Chettle to go one better with his second attempt.

Nigel Jemson then wasted a chance to make it 2–0 and by this point Derby had already been forced into an early change with youngster Craig Ramage replacing the injured Geraint Williams after only eight minutes.

It proved to be a great move. Just two minutes after Forest went ahead, a neat pass slid in from the right and Ramage moved on to it before cleverly lifting his shot over the out-rushing Mark Crossley with a smart little chip past the prone stopper.

Amazingly, that was Derby's first goal at home to Forest in the League since the famous 4–1 over the then-European champions back in 1979.

From there the game was always going to be a battle and it would be about who was able to wrestle the upper-hand away from their rivals first.

Mark Wright threatened for the Rams with a header that hit the bar after he met Nigel Callaghan's free-kick, while at the other end Wright was magnificent in his more familiar defensive duty, aided by Mark Patterson and Nick Pickering – the pair only playing with Derby suffering a lack of available full-backs.

The match's crucial moment arrived on the hour mark with relative simplicity allied to great celebrations among the home faithful.

Mick Harford won a ball in the air and nodded it out to the right where Gary Micklewhite was waiting, and his delightful ball in was met by a powerful header from Dean Saunders that left Crossley totally beaten.

Holding on to the advantage became Derby's next ambition and they managed to do so without any real alarms, save for Peter Shilton making a fairly straightforward stop from Nigel Clough.

Derby's players had given everything and restored pride after the previous week's hammering at Leeds by not only beating their local rivals, but by lifting themselves up to 17th in the table too.

Derby: Shilton, Patterson, Pickering, G. Williams (Ramage 8), Wright, Forsyth, Micklewhite, Saunders, Harford, Hebberd, Callaghan.

Other Sub: Kavanagh

Forest: Crossley, Laws, Pearce, Walker, Chettle, Hodge (Starbuck 69), Crosby, Keane, Clough, Jemson, Parker.

Other Sub: Wassall

Referee: C. Trussell

Attendance: 21,729

Reaction

'DALGLISH STYLE FROM RAMAGE' exclaimed the headline on the back of the *Derby Telegraph* in relation to the Rams' first goal.

And it was a fair point as the young midfielder's turn inside the Forest box and chipped finish over goalkeeper Mark Crossley was reminiscent of a move that Dalglish had employed when scoring the goal to win Liverpool's second European Cup in 1978.

Ramage had been introduced as an early substitute for the injured Geraint Williams having been given a rest from the starting line-up following the previous week's 3–0 defeat at Leeds.

Manager Arthur Cox was pleased with Ramage's response and said after the game: 'Craig took his chance like Kenny Dalglish, a little chip when the goalkeeper committed himself.

'But he owed the other lads a goal because he has missed a number of chances this season.

'There are some very good and competitive players in both teams and we deserved to win because we were always that little bit more of a threat.

'Dean Saunders scored an excellent goal and Micky Harford always troubled Forest. Mark Wright was magnificent and the two full-backs were very effective.

'We had a good week preparing for Forest and the players were aware that we would have our backs to the wall if we lost. Instead, we have beaten a good side and we should take strength from that.'

And while it was Ramage who sparked the comeback, equalising shortly after Derby went behind, the head of Dean Saunders supplied the winning goal in the second half with a towering effort in front of the Normanton End.

Saunders had praise for Ramage and also for winger Gary Micklewhite, who had played a big part in both goals.

Saunders said: 'Gary Micklewhite was involved in both goals and is in a purple patch. He has come back unbelievably well after a bad knee injury and looks better than ever.

'I think the doctors must have put an extra spring in his knee and his cross for my goal was perfect. I don't score many with my head but all I had to do was make sure I got a good strike on the ball.

'Craig showed his class by the way he took his goal. If people allow him to get on with his game, we may have a player in who will be worth millions in the future.'

But the final words must go to Graham Richards, the BBC Radio Derby commentator who called Saunders' goal with his usual gusto for a sequence of words that became iconic among Rams fans.

'Micklewhite thumps it over, early ball, up goes Saunders…GOAL! GOAL! GOAL! 2–1 Derby County! What a header! Forest are behind! Dig that one out of the net Mark Crossley, not a chance! In the back! 2–1!'

What Happened Next

Victory over your local rivals can be a bit of a spark for your season but in this case it was a continuation of a good recent run of form that Derby had embarked on after an awful start to their season.

Prior to the Forest match they had been six games unbeaten only to see their run ended by a 3–0 defeat at Leeds that manager Arthur Cox had looked to use as motivation when preparing for the visit of the Reds.

And once Forest had been seen off, the Rams did back it up over the next couple of matches, drawing 1–1 away to Sheffield Wednesday in the League Cup before winning 2–1 away to Sunderland.

But that is pretty much where the positives for the 1990–91 season came to an end. The League Cup replay at home to Sheffield Wednesday saw the underdogs triumph, the Second Division Owls claiming a 2–1 win at the Baseball Ground, and in Derby's next First Division match they were beaten 6–4 at home to Chelsea.

The momentum that Derby had created in their run of one defeat in 10 fixtures was quickly extinguished as it became apparent that they would be suffering another season of relegation trouble.

Little did anyone know that the win at Sunderland would not be followed up by another victory until the following May, when Southampton were beaten 6–2 at the Baseball Ground in the third to last game of the season, by which time the fate of Cox's men had been confirmed.

Derby had been doomed for some time before they went to Manchester City on 20 April and lost 2–1, Dean Saunders seeing his penalty saved by City striker Niall Quinn who was in goal after Tony Coton was sent off.

The result confirmed Derby's relegation to the Second Division, although they did have one last positive with that win against Southampton to end a run of 20 games without a victory – a record that stood until the 2007–08 Premier League campaign.

Robert Maxwell eventually departed the Baseball Ground in the summer of 1991, freeing Derby of the shackles they had operated under during the last couple of years of his chairmanship, with first Brian Fearn and then Lionel Pickering taking over.

As for Forest, they were a little inconsistent after the defeat but recovered to finish eighth but lost to Tottenham Hotspur in the FA Cup Final, the only Final of the competition that Brian Clough took part in – it remained the only honour he failed to win during his career.

Featured Player

As the club's first £1 million signing, Dean Saunders was definitely a bold move by Derby County but he more than repaid his record-breaking fee.

He had been signed in October 1988 from Oxford United and immediately set about showing his worth to the Derby faithful with two goals on his debut, a 4–1 victory at home to Wimbledon.

Swansea-born Saunders scored 14 goals in 30 First Division games in his first season at the Baseball Ground, helping Derby to finish fifth and forming an excellent partnership with Paul Goddard, the clever Englishman a perfect foil for the explosive Welshman.

Hopes were high that Derby could push on the following season but the sale of Goddard to Millwall midway through 1989–90 was the first sign that the Rams were not going to be progressing as they had looked like they might.

Derby struggled in that 1989–90 campaign, although they did reach the quarter-final of the League Cup, and Saunders only notched 11 First Division goals, but he was on his best form in 1990–91 with 17 League goals and the Rams' Player of the Year award.

Unfortunately, that was also the season that saw Derby relegated from the top-flight and it was no surprise to see England's top clubs after the number eight, who eventually moved to Liverpool in a double deal with skipper Mark Wright having scored 57 goals in 131 games.

Saunders was not eligible for a League Cup tie a few days after his debut but otherwise he never missed a match for the Rams, making 130 consecutive appearances.

He spent a year with Liverpool before moving to Aston Villa, and in 1995–96 he played in Turkey with Galatasaray then returned to England to sign for Nottingham Forest.

Naturally, Saunders then scored for Forest against Derby in that season's Premier League meeting at the City Ground, and in the return at the Baseball Ground he received a great reception from the home faithful.

Spells with Sheffield United and Benfica followed, and Saunders returned to the Premier League with Bradford City in 1999 at the age of 35 and again was handed a brilliant ovation when lining up against Derby, this time at Pride Park Stadium.

Saunders coached at Bradford, Blackburn Rovers and Newcastle United, became assistant manager for the Wales national side in 2007, took over as boss of Wrexham a year later, and in September 2011 moved up to the Championship to take charge of Doncaster Rovers.

His playing career had started in 1982 with home team Swansea City and he later had a loan spell with Cardiff City before moving to Brighton & Hove Albion and then on to Oxford.

Derby County 3 Nottingham Forest 2

8 September 1993

Background

Derby County v Nottingham Forest in European competition – yes, you are reading this correctly, it did actually happen.

It was not, however, the European Cup, which both sides had enjoyed success in under Brian Clough, who guided the Rams to the 1973 semi-finals then took Forest to consecutive victories in 1979 and 1980.

It was not even the old UEFA Cup, in which Forest had reached the semi-finals under Clough in 1984 only to exit at the hands of Anderlecht in controversial circumstances reminiscent of Derby's defeat to Juventus in 1973.

Instead it was the Anglo-Italian Cup, which had been reintroduced to English football ready for the 1992–93 season as a replacement for the Full Members Cup, abolished after the advent of the Premier League.

The competition was open only to teams from the two countries' respective second tiers – Italy's Serie B and England's newly structured Division One, in which Derby were playing their football with Forest still in the top-flight.

And with the tournament set up to guarantee a representative from each country in the final at Wembley, the Rams took their chance to go all the way and fought their way through to the national stadium only to lose 3–1 to Cremonese with Marco Gabbiadini scoring their goal and goalkeeper Martin Taylor saving a penalty.

As an aside, Derby had not been the county's first representatives in the Anglo-Italian Cup – Matlock Town had finished as English runners-up in 1979, when the tournament was open only to non-League clubs.

But back to the modern variation of the competition, and by the time the 1993–94 season came around the qualifying stages had been given a bit of a shake-up and the English teams placed in preliminary regional groups.

Forest's relegation from the Premier League at the end of 1992–93 meant they came into the equation and when the groups were revealed the Rams and their big rivals had been drawn together, along with Notts County, with each team to play each other once.

Clough's retirement from the City Ground hot-seat ended the main link between the two sides' previous European successes but the draw had created the mouth-watering prospect of the meeting at the Baseball Ground.

Derby had lost their first game in the competition, 3–2 away to Notts County, and knew they needed to beat Forest to stand any chance of progressing to the next stage.

And Arthur Cox's expensively assembled team went in on the back of an abysmal performance in losing 3–0 at Birmingham City four days previously, a second reverse by that scoreline in the space of three matches.

'Derby County go on trial,' reported the *Derby Telegraph*, adding 'even if they beat Forest the jury will still be sitting' and 'the beating at St Andrew's shook public confidence'.

Cox was absent from his duties because of a back complaint so assistant manager Roy McFarland spoke ahead of the game and said: 'We have to show more pride than against Birmingham.

'For me and all the players involved on Saturday, the sooner the next game came around, the better.

'That's all we have been waiting for. The fact that it's Forest makes it ideal.'

Recent signing John Harkes was a doubt for the Rams because of a knee injury but former Red Darren Wassall was set to return after suspension, while the visitors were expected to include new £2 million striker Stan Collymore for only his second competitive start for the club.

It was the second meeting between Derby and Forest already in the season following on from a 1–1 draw at the City Ground in August.

Report

A goalless first half gave no real indication of what was to come on a wet night at the Baseball Ground as the two old rivals met for the second time in the space of a few weeks.

Forest should have been clear in the opening 45 minutes as they enjoyed the better of proceedings with Derby 'keeper Martin Taylor making several good saves.

He produced good stops from Lee Glover and Robert Rosario, while Steve Stone wasted a good opportunity when he capitalised on some poor play by Gary Charles – the Rams again showing the slackness in defence that had cost them dearly in recent matches.

Conditions were hardly good for flowing football but both sets of players battled their way through it, though the first half also produced four yellow cards with lively challenges flying that were appropriate to the occasion.

Forest eventually took the lead three minutes after the break through Glover, whose shot skipped up off the wet turf and bounced over the diving Taylor, and the scorer then saw one cleared off the line by Martin Kuhl.

Craig Short's mistake on 52 minutes saw the visitors double their lead through Scot Gemmill and Derby once again had Taylor to thank for fine saves from Rosario and Ian Woan.

The turning point arrived on 67 when Forest debutant Steve Blatherwick caught Paul Kitson with a high challenge and up stepped Paul Simpson to score following the resulting free-kick with his first goal of the season.

Two minutes later the Rams were level thanks to Kitson's fine finish but they were soon almost behind again, Woan forcing another save from Taylor.

And Derby saved their best moment until three minutes from time. Blatherwick headed Simpson's corner out to Kuhl, who took aim from just outside the box with a low shot that beat the efforts of Lyttle who did his best to get it clear.

Derby's comeback was complete, much to the delight of the fans who had braved the elements to be at the Baseball Ground.

Derby: Taylor, Charles, Forsyth, Kuhl, Short, Wassall, Johnson, Williams, Kitson, Gabbiadini, Simpson.

Subs: Sutton (GK), Chalk, Kavanagh

Forest: Crossley, Little, Laws, Blatherwick, Chettle, Stone, Gemmill, Glover (McGregor 85), Rosario, Collymore, Woan.

Other Subs: Marriott (GK), McKinnon

Referee: V. Callow

Booked: Kuhl, Williams (Derby); Laws, Rosario (Forest)

Attendance: 6,654

Reaction

It may not have been the Baseball Ground's biggest crowd or the biggest match to have ever been played between the two sides, but any victory for the Rams over Forest is always one to savour.

And when it comes with a late winner to cap a comeback from 2–0 down it is even sweeter and the players certainly enjoyed it, as demonstrated by the celebratory picture on the back of the following day's *Derby Telegraph*.

Derby's crucial third goal had arrived from the right boot of skipper Martin Kuhl, a low drive in front of the Normanton End, and the midfielder earned praise from assistant manager Roy McFarland.

Speaking after the game, he said: 'I was pleased for Martin because he rallied us when we went 2–0 down.

'He was the inspiration behind our recovery and has set his standards. He has to maintain them but we could do without him being booked in every game. We want him competing in midfield not sitting out a suspension.

'It was an important result for us because it was the next game after Birmingham. There was some character on display, which was important after Saturday, and more commitment.

'I felt for the players when they went 2–0 down but we have talked about individual mistakes and Craig Short gave us another example for Forest's second goal.

'Martin Taylor made some good saves, especially from Ian Woan's left foot, and Marco Gabbiadini gave us more than he did on Saturday. He can give us more still.'

Tommy Johnson, a late inclusion in the Rams' starting line-up, added: 'We got stuck in at the end of the second half and caused problems by running at them. Perhaps they thought the game was won because they laid back for a spell.'

But while there were smiles in the Derby dressing room, the mood was not so positive in the Forest camp with manager Frank Clark fuming at his players for 'absolutely, totally and utterly throwing away the tie'.

He concluded: 'At 2–0 we had the game won but then played without control or discipline.'

What Happened Next

A pair of 3–2 wins in the group's opening two fixtures, with one game still to go, meant that any one of the three teams could make it through to the next stage.

Having played twice, Derby's chances of progressing were out of their own hands and it was down to the Nottingham Forest v Notts County match the following week to decide who would come out on top.

There was a very real possibility of all three teams ending up with the same points, goal difference and away goals, which were the three deciding factors in the group standings, should Forest beat County 3–2, and if that had have happened lots would be drawn to decide the group winners.

In the end County progressed on the back of a 1–1 draw at Forest, and ultimately went all the way to Wembley where they lost to a Brescia side that included Gheorghe Hagi.

But the main focus was on Division One where Forest would eventually finish as runners-up to Crystal Palace and earn an immediate return to the Premier League, where Derby were hoping to follow.

Relegated in 1991, Derby lost in the Play-offs the following year and reached the Play-offs again this time around having finished sixth, and after easing through the semi-final against Millwall they faced Leicester City at Wembley for a place in the top-flight.

Tommy Johnson's goal put them in front midway through the first half and on their way, only for Steve Walsh's controversial equaliser – coming after a foul on Martin Taylor was missed – levelled matters before half-time.

And with just a few minutes left, John Harkes missed a sitter for Derby that proved crucial as the Foxes poured forward and Walsh stabbed in the winning goal, clinching promotion for his side after two successive defeats in the Final at Wembley and condemning Derby to another year in the First Division.

As for the Anglo-Italian Cup, Notts County reached the Final again in 1995 and were victorious against Ascoli before it was scrapped in 1996 because the two countries could not agree on dates for fixtures, and also with increased violence at games.

Genoa beat Port Vale 5–2 in the final Final with Derby having chosen not to enter that last staging of the competition.

Featured Player

Martin Kuhl might have scored the winning goal in this thriller while 'keeper Martin Taylor produced some fine stops to preserve the Rams' advantage – but none of that would have been possible had one man not stepped up to the plate with a wave of his trusty left foot to spark it all off.

Paul Simpson had struggled to really nail down a place in Derby's line-up so far in 1993–94 but on that rainy September night he well and truly showed his worth.

He started wearing the number 11 shirt and it was his precise strike in the 67th minute that got Derby back in the game from 2–0 down and allowed them to quickly level before winning the match in the last minute.

It was a typically Simpson goal and a sight seen by Derby fans many times during his five years with the club.

Signed from Oxford United for £500,000 in February 1992, Simpson had already been an impressive player for Manchester City – where he started his career – and Oxford, earning himself England Under-21 caps along the way.

He was a part of Lionel Pickering's big-money revolution at the Baseball Ground but at a mere half-million he cost a lot less than many of his contemporaries and certainly offered value for money.

Simpson quickly made himself a fan favourite with his performances on the left-wing, adding style and class to the position along with plenty of goals and assists.

The 1993 Anglo-Italian Cup Final gave him the chance to appear for Derby at Wembley and he repeated the feat a year later in the Play-off Final, when the Rams missed out on a place in the Premier League.

He had been signed by Arthur Cox but Roy McFarland also saw Simpson's value to the team after taking over and in January 1995 came one of the winger's highlights in a Derby shirt, scoring a stunning hat-trick against Portsmouth in a 3–0 win that contributed towards Jim Smith losing his job at Pompey.

Smith was installed at Derby the following summer and got plenty out of Simpson, who – in a variety of roles – reached double figures for goals and set up both in the 2–1 win against Crystal Palace that secured promotion.

The Premier League was the beginning of the end of Simpson's Derby career, although he scored in the dramatic 3–3 draw at home to Leeds United on the opening day and made 19 substitute appearances in that first season up.

His final appearance came from the bench in a 5–0 win over Southend United in the League Cup in October 1997 and Simpson then left for Wolverhampton Wanderers having made 225 appearances for the club, scoring 57 goals.

Simpson later played for Walsall, Blackpool, Rochdale and Carlisle United, the latter two in a player-manager capacity, before hanging up his boots in 2006 and becoming manager at Preston North End having led Carlisle to two successive promotions.

Later to manage Shrewsbury Town and Stockport County, Simpson scored a hat-trick against Tranmere Rovers in April 1996 that – at the time of writing – was the last one by a Rams player in a League fixture, some 16 years ago.

He was named as manager of Evo-Stik Northern Premier League side Northwich Victoria in January 2012 with another ex-Ram – former on-loan defender Alan Wright – as his assistant, but Simpson only stayed for a month before going to coach in Portugal.

Nottingham Forest 1 Derby County 1

19 October 1996

Background

Derby County and Nottingham Forest had met previously in the top division of English football but a lot had changed since their last encounter, April 1991 in the old Division One.

For use of the word 'old' had become common-place in the intervening years following the innovation of the Premier League in 1992, when the top clubs of the 'old' Division One broke away from the Football League to start their own elite competition, and – if you believe a lot of modern-day supporters – football in England began.

Forest were among that group of clubs to compete in the first season of the Premier League and actually earned themselves a place in the history books when Teddy Sheringham scored the first goal in the Premier League televised live on Sky Sports.

Derby, on the other hand, had missed out when losing to Blackburn Rovers in the Play-off semi-final in 1992, while the Reds lasted just one season in the new division before being relegated at the end of that inaugural campaign.

They had bounced straight back in 1994, finished third in 1995, and reached the quarter-final of the UEFA Cup in 1996, the same season that saw Derby finally earn their place in what was seen by many as the 'promised land' of the Premier League.

So the release of the fixtures was hotly anticipated and a first meeting between the two teams was scheduled for 19 October at the City Ground, the 3pm Saturday kick-off remaining in place with no movement for TV coverage or police advice.

And even though only a little over five years had passed since the last top-flight game the sides played against each other, the football landscape had changed with the advent of the Premier League with vast sums of money now in the game, worldwide interest, and even smaller things such as squad numbers on players' shirts.

Derby had taken to Premier League life reasonably well after their promotion, although by the time they prepared for their visit to the City Ground they had only won twice since the season's opening weekend – in consecutive fixtures at the start of September.

But on the other side of the coin they had only been beaten three times with two of those defeats – at home to Wimbledon then Newcastle United – coming in the two fixtures immediately prior to the Forest trip.

Forest, meanwhile, were desperately lacking in form having not won a Premier League game since triumphing away to Coventry City on the opening day, and they too went in on the back of a defeat having been beaten 2–0 at Leeds United seven days before this fixture.

Derby were looking for the points to boost their Premier League campaign while they were also looking to break a hoodoo that had lasted almost 25 years – not since 30 October 1971 had they won at the City Ground.

Manager Jim Smith was aware of that fact as he prepared his team and speaking in advance of the short journey along the A52 he said: 'If we draw against Manchester United or lose to Newcastle United at home, I think supporters can handle that. Provided our performance is reasonable, they will accept results like that.

'Playing Forest is different. Supporters just cannot countenance defeat in this one. We want to win for them but also because three points would give us some breathing space. We have to keep believing in our ability and not be sucked down among the nervous clubs.

'Forest want the points for the same reason. We would rather be up at the top together – or on our own – but the reality is that we need points after two home defeats.'

The Premier League table had Forest fourth from bottom with seven points while Derby were three places and three points further on with both sides having played 10 games.

Derby also had striking concerns with their lack of recent goals, along with an injury to Dean Sturridge and Marco Gabbiadini's loan to Birmingham City, while Dutchman Ron Willems was back in the squad.

With that in mind, the bookmakers offered odds of 6-1 on the joint favourites to be the game's first goalscorer – Forest duo Kevin Campbell and Dean Saunders, set to play against Derby for the first time since leaving them in 1991 for Liverpool.

Report

There is always an argument that if you cannot win a game of football you make sure you do not lose it, so in that sense the Rams' 1–1 draw at Nottingham Forest was definitely a tick in the positive column.

Any game on the turf of your local rivals is always going to be a tight affair so the worst thing you can possibly do is go a goal behind with just 73 seconds on the clock.

And in some instances stories are already written. This was one of them as Dean Saunders, back in English football with Nottingham Forest after a spell with Galatasaray in Turkey, lined up against Derby for the first time since leaving the Baseball Ground for Liverpool in 1991 – and scored the opening goal of the game.

That it came so early in proceedings, and in front of the massed Derby fans at the City Ground, only served to rub salt in the wounds.

Saunders finished well from Jason Lee's cross and could have added a second before the break as the Rams struggled to really assert themselves on the game with their attacks regularly coming to nothing.

But a Forest side devoid of confidence could not take advantage and stretch their lead either, though early in the second half Saunders once again came close to notching against his old club.

And Jim Smith's side made them pay on the hour through Christian Dailly's composed finish from inside the penalty area as he rolled the ball past Mark Crossley after Aljosa Asanovic had been challenged and gone down looking for a penalty having collected a knock-down from Ron Willems.

Dailly's intervention meant referee Jeff Winter did not have time to make a decision, and from there the Rams might have won it; first when Ian Woan sliced a clearance off his own post then Ashley Ward shot over after carving out a chance for himself.

Equally, they might have lost it. Saunders sniffed yet another opportunity, while Russell Hoult saved well from Bryan Roy to ensure that the points were shared in this first-ever Premier League meeting between the two sides.

Forest: Crossley, Cooper, Blatherwick, Pearce (Chettle HT), Lyttle, Bart-Williams, Woan, Gemmill (Roy 70), Allen, Saunders, Lee.

Other Subs: Fettis (GK), Haaland, Guinan

Derby: Hoult, Rowett, McGrath, Stimac, Laursen (Carsley 64), Dailly, D. Powell, C. Powell, Asanovic, Willems (Simpson 88), Ward (Carbon 79).

Other Subs: Flynn, Quy (GK)

Referee: J. Winter

Booked: Gemmill, Lee, Lyttle, Crossley (Forest); Laursen, Stimac (Derby)

Attendance: 27,771

Reaction

Coming from behind to take a point against your local rivals, especially having recovered from the setback of conceding in the second minute, can never be classed as a bad result – particularly in the ultra-competitive world of the Premier League.

That was certainly the feeling among the Baseball Ground faithful after Derby took their Premier League points tally to 11 from 10 games with the hard-earned 1-1 draw at the City Ground.

Young Scottish midfielder Christian Dailly was the subject of media interest after the game having earned the Rams a point with his second goal since his summer arrival from Dundee United.

It was Derby's first goal in the Premier League since a 1–0 win over Sunderland on September 14 and earned them a vital point – not that the press were able to catch up with Dailly quickly.

He had been selected for a random drug test after the final whistle, alongside Darryl Powell and Forest duo Des Lyttle and Jason Lee, and was not able to do any interviews for more than 90 minutes as a result.

But the press were patient and when Dailly was finally able to speak, he admitted: 'Most teams are happy with an away point but we feel we could have taken more from the game. Forest probably think it's a fair result because they had some chances too.

'This was my first local derby here and while it was tense, it was an open game. I'm pleased with a goal and we created quite a lot. Some will say that a goal from midfield takes some pressure off the strikers – but if they score it takes pressure off us.

'Ashley Ward was unlucky not to have a goal because he held off two defenders so well but we'll keep working at it.'

And while Dailly had netted his second goal for Derby, scoring his second goal for Forest was Dean Saunders – within a couple of minutes of starting his first game against the club that he had scored over 50 goals for between 1988 and 1991.

'I was probably fated to score' admitted Saunders. 'But I could have had a hat-trick.

'We had a few chances but Derby had most of the game and definitely deserved a draw. They passed it around nicely at times and look a decent side.

'We're not playing with any confidence, although any team would miss Steve Stone. We've had Kevin Campbell out and Stuart Pearce went off with a back injury. Manchester United or Liverpool might be able to stand losing three players of that calibre but we can't.'

What Happened Next

Derby's next fixture saw them lose 2–1 away to a Robbie Fowler-inspired Liverpool in front of the Sky Sports cameras a week later but the start of November saw them embark on a run of form that really lifted them up the table.

Leicester City were beaten at the Baseball Ground, as were Middlesbrough in the next match – again screened live on Sky – then the upturn continued on 23 November when they headed to West Ham United and came back with a point from a 1–1 draw earned thanks to Dean Sturridge's excellent goal.

Derby had shown resilience to come from behind in East London and they demonstrated patience a week later when facing Coventry City at home, where Ashley Ward netted a late winner to make it three from four for the month.

It was almost four from five at the start of December when Derby were seconds away from winning 2–1 at Arsenal, a game notable for Sturridge's stunning turn and shot in off the bar, but fortunes can turn quickly in the Premier League and perhaps that late blow knocked the players back.

Derby were not victorious again until January when winning at Gillingham in the FA Cup, a result quickly followed by a home beating of Aston Villa in the same competition, but three more Premier League points did not arrive until 15 February when an Aljosa Asanovic penalty saw off West Ham – ending a run of nine games without a win.

It was not a result that 'saved' Derby's season but it gave them fresh impetus after a difficult few months and from that point they were never in serious relegation danger as they picked up results regularly, including notable wins over Chelsea, Tottenham Hotspur, Manchester United and Aston Villa.

Forest's poor form continued after the draw with five defeats in seven games, prompting a change of manager as Frank Clark left the hot seat while Stuart Pearce was put in as caretaker while continuing his playing duties, and for a while that move looked like paying off.

Forest won their first game under Pearce, beating Arsenal at the City Ground on 21 December, then they started 1997 by winning five on the spin – including two FA Cup ties – to give them hope of getting out of trouble.

Their FA Cup ambitions were ended in the fifth round by Chesterfield, in the Spireites' remarkable run to the semi-final, but Forest's inability to win Premier League matches – they drew four on the spin in March – was costing them dearly as they could not drag themselves out of trouble.

A 1–1 stalemate at home to Leeds United on April 19 was a fifth single-pointer in six, by which time Forest and Derby were ready for the return fixture at the City Ground.

Featured Player

Not a huge amount was known about Christian Dailly when Jim Smith went shopping north of the border in the summer of 1996 to bring him to the Baseball Ground from Dundee United.

Dailly was only 22, despite having already appeared more than 170 times for his home-town club Dundee United making his first-team debut at the age of 16 in August 1990.

He had a reputation for being a talented young midfielder with great energy, the ability to get up and down the field at will, and with an eye for goal, while also having the versatility to slot in at centre-half if required.

Dailly was already a Scottish Under-21 international and moved to Derby for £500,000 with the same amount payable again if he went on to achieve full international honours while at the Baseball Ground – which he did.

Derby certainly got their money's worth as he proved quickly to be a shrewd capture, scoring his first goal in only his second appearance to earn a stoppage-time point away at Tottenham Hotspur, and showing himself to be more than at home in English football.

His goal against Forest was the second of three that season with his third coming in a pre-Christmas defeat at Southampton when he was used as a secondary striker – showing the versatility that would come in handy just a month later.

A pre-match injury to Jacob Laursen ahead of an FA Cup tie at home to Aston Villa saw Dailly shifted back to centre-half, where he gave a performance so outstanding that he spent pretty much the rest of his Derby career in defence rather than midfield.

His performances helped establish Derby in the Premier League in 1996–97 then push them on further the following year to finish ninth, and after a clean sheet at Blackburn Rovers on the opening day of 1998–99 Dailly was on the move – to Rovers for £5.3 million, at the time the Rams' record incoming fee.

Dailly had played 78 games for Derby and made his international debut as a Ram before his move to Blackburn, where he spent two and a half years before a switch to West Ham United.

He helped the Hammers win promotion from the Championship and played in the 2006 FA Cup final before a loan move to Southampton, a return to Scotland with Rangers for 18 months, and the 2009–10 and 2010–11 seasons with Charlton Athletic.

Dailly also won 67 caps for Scotland but his career was not over and he moved to Portsmouth on a short-term deal at the start of 2011–12, appearing twice for the Fratton Park club then later joined Southend United.

Derby County 0 Nottingham Forest 0

23 April 1997

Background

The business end of the 1996–97 Premier League season was well and truly upon us by the time this fixture between the two great rivals came around.

Survival was certainly the name of the game with the two clubs having vastly different chances of remaining in the top-flight.

The fixture arrived five days short of a year since Derby had won promotion so memorably against Crystal Palace and, in what was their first venture into the new Premier League, they were looking well set to finish comfortably clear of relegation danger.

They went in to the game 12th on 42 points, seven points clear of the relegation zone and with only three fixtures remaining – Forest, away to struggling Coventry City, then at home to Arsenal on the final day.

Forest, on the other hand, were in deep trouble after a turbulent season that had seen previous boss Frank Clark replaced by defender Stuart Pearce and the experienced Dave Bassett and were bottom, five points from safety also with three games to go.

Derby manager Jim Smith had already announced his intention to change goalkeeper after Russell Hoult's poor run of form, with Mart Poom to return – if fit – or Martin Taylor to take over for what would be the Baseball Ground's final competitive floodlit game before the summer move to Pride Park.

And while focused on the victory he felt would ensure survival, Smith was also well aware of what the game meant as he prepared to take charge of Derby against Forest for the second time after the 1–1 draw at the City Ground earlier in the season.

He said: 'The expectations of the fans are very high. There will be no problem in getting our players going because we're at home, a floodlit game has its own atmosphere and Forest are the visitors.

'It will be tough. Forest have nothing to lose and simply have to go for victory in all their last three games.

'Three points for us would nail it. We feel we're safe but there's always a little doubt until it's certain.'

Forest knew that it was do or die if they were to give their faint hopes of staying up a shot in the arm and in Pearce's eyes, Derby away was as good a fixture as they could have wished for given their plight.

He said: 'Derby is one of the best places we could go at this time. It means a lot to the players and, especially, to the supporters.

'Anybody who has been at this club more than a year knows the importance of this fixture.'

The encounter also marked the first playing return to the Baseball Ground of Dean Saunders, who had left Derby in the summer of 1991 for Liverpool having enjoyed three prolific seasons in the Rams' number eight shirt.

Saunders had scored in the reverse fixture at the City Ground earlier in the season and was looking forward to coming back – while he was also full of praise for Paul McGrath, the Rams' October signing from Aston Villa.

Saunders said of his former Villa colleague: 'Paul is a class player and I've never seen him have a bad game.

'Almost single-handedly in December and January, he kept them (Derby) up. Derby needed somebody with Paul's experience and it was an inspired signing by Jim Smith.'

As an aside, in the days leading up to this fixture the *Derby Telegraph* had carried a story on Lance Corporal Richard Bagshaw, who was from Borrowash but was stationed out in Bosnia on duty with the forces.

He was appealing for Derby County memorabilia and pictures to put up in his living quarters – which he shared with Nottingham Forest fans!

Report

A failure to take advantage of opportunities when they arrived was the downfall of both teams in this encounter and led to a hard-fought goalless draw, albeit one without any real great chances.

Both sides hit the woodwork in a tight opening 45 minutes with Derby's Paulo Wanchope, who had been called in for only his second start, coming the closest.

He rose to meet Jacob Laursen's delightful free-kick with a powerful downward header that bounced up and hit the bar, leading boss Jim Smith to later say: 'It's as if there's concrete under the surface, the way the ball bounced.'

At the other end, Forest's Steve Chettle pushed forward from the back and let fly from 30 yards with a shot that hit the top of the bar, although it never really caused Martin Taylor any serious danger.

Taylor was back at Derby after a loan spell with Wycombe Wanderers and with Mart Poom injured and Russell Hoult in poor form, he was back in the starting line-up.

He responded with a solid performance on a night in which he did not have a lot to do, but when he was called into action he came up with the goods.

Taylor dived well at the feet of Pierre van Hooijdonk and Alf Inge Haaland, while also watching efforts from van Hooijdonk and former Ram Dean Saunders sail wide of the target.

Forest went in to the game desperate for a win to keep them in the fight to stay up and pushed men forward late on in a bid to find a goal but that only served to let Derby in.

Dean Sturridge had a couple of good opportunities, and right at the death Robin van der Laan had his eyes on a very late winning goal but was denied by Forest 'keeper Alan Fettis.

There had not been much between the two sides across the 90 minutes and a draw was perhaps the fairest result. It was certainly one that helped Derby more than it did their visitors.

Derby: Taylor, Rowett, Larsen, Dailly, Carsley, van der Laan, Trollope, Asanovic, C. Powell, Wanchope (Ward 79), Sturridge.

Subs: Hoult (GK), Willems, Simpson, Solis

Forest: Fettis, Phillips, Warner, Chettle, Lyttle, O'Neil, Gemmill (Moore 83), Woan (Haaland 69), Allen, Saunders, van Hooijdonk.

Other Subs: Henry (GK), Smith, Burns

Referee: G. Poll

Booked: Sturridge (Derby); O'Neil, Gemmill, van Hooijdonk (Forest)

Attendance: 18,087

Reaction

With the game ending goalless, neither manager was particularly thrilled by the result. Derby manager Jim Smith certainly felt his side should have won on the night having had by far the better of the opportunities and the possession.

'It was a typical local derby, all battle,' said Smith. 'But the amount of the ball we had we should have brought victory.

'At the end, when Forest shoved everybody forward, we had two or three good chances to settle it. But it was down to the same thing, a shortage of composure.'

Smith had given Costa Rican striker Paulo Wanchope his second start, following his remarkable debut goal at Manchester United earlier in the month, and the 20-year-old had come as close as anyone to scoring with a downward header that bounced up and hit the bar.

It was Wanchope's first experience of such a local derby occasion and Smith backed him to learn from it, while also praising his defence – including recalled goalkeeper Martin Taylor.

'What he (Taylor) was asked to do, he did very well. He went down bravely at people's feet – but courage has never been a problem.

'The back three were good. Paul McGrath was suffering from an Achilles tendon problem but Gary Rowett, Jacob Laursen and Christian Dailly did extremely well.'

The result left Forest in even deeper trouble, still bottom of the table but with two games to go and five points away from having a chance of staying up.

General manager Dave Bassett admitted after the match that the club's destiny was not in their own hands and added: 'We need some freak results or absolute miracles if we are to stay up and we needed three points off Derby.

'With a bit of luck near the end we might have got the extra two points, without necessarily deserving them. Draws are not much use to us.

'In mid-season it's a good performance to draw a local derby away but at this stage we need more.

'Since I came in we've never scored more than one goal in a game. Not enough is being created but teams with somebody who can score 20 goals don't get relegated.'

It all meant that Forest were on the verge of relegation while Derby were on the verge of safety, sitting 11th and six points clear of the drop-zone.

And Smith added: 'To me, it looks like the three clubs going down will end up with something like 38, 39 and 40 points.'

What Happened Next

Derby knew they were almost safe, a tremendous feat in what was their debut season in the Premier League, and although they had to wait 10 days for their next match they wrapped everything up at the next opportunity.

They began in May with an away fixture at Coventry City, who were fighting for their own life and sat fourth from bottom as the two teams met at Highfield Road.

A Gary Rowett goal put Derby in front four minutes after half-time, Gary McAllister levelled it 10 minutes later, but Dean Sturridge's fine turn and finish on 67 was enough to secure a 2–1 win for Smith's side and confirm their safety in the Premier League – not that, over the season, it had ever been in any real doubt.

And if that was not enough for the Derby fans to celebrate, the day also saw Forest's return to the First Division confirmed.

Rams fans could be heard singing 'going down at the Baseball Ground' and 'we'll never play you again' during the 0–0 draw against Forest but while relegation did not happen then, it did at the start of May.

Forest needed to win at home to Wimbledon to stand any chance of staying up, and even then results elsewhere would have to go in their favour, but the bottom side could only muster a 1–1 draw as their hopes of survival were finally extinguished.

Middlesbrough and Sunderland joined them on the final day after Coventry produced their own great escape by winning at Tottenham Hotspur.

Forest closed their season by going down 5–0 at Newcastle United and Derby were also beaten, 3–1 at home to Arsenal, although the result was not as important as the occasion – the final competitive game at the Baseball Ground, the Rams' home for more than a century before the move to Pride Park.

Featured Player

Although nobody knew for sure at the time, the 0–0 draw against Forest would prove to be goalkeeper Martin Taylor's last competitive appearance in a Derby shirt.

Fittingly, he kept a clean sheet and earned praise for his performance against his club's greatest rivals and if there was a way for him to sign off as a Ram, this was probably it.

There was a time when it looked like Taylor would never even play again after he suffered a horrendous broken leg in a televised game at Southend United in October 1994.

Typical of the man, even while down injured he managed to scramble the ball away to safety before he found his career on hold.

Taylor did not play another professional game until September 1996, on loan at Crewe Alexandra, and was often on the bench for the Rams in their debut Premier

League season before making his Derby comeback in March 1997 in an FA Cup quarter-final at home to Middlesbrough.

He played in a couple of Premier League games before the arrival of Mart Poom limited his chances of re-establishing himself in the first team and was loaned to Wycombe Wanderers for a month before returning to the Baseball Ground, where an injury to Poom and the loss of form of Russell Hoult saw him recalled to face Forest.

Taylor was on the bench at Coventry City 10 days later for his final senior involvement for Derby before his time as a Ram eventually came to an end on an emotional night at the Baseball Ground with a testimonial match against Everton.

Signed from non-League side Mile Oak Rovers in 1986, it took Taylor some years to really establish himself in Derby's first team as he made fleeting appearances here and there with Peter Shilton firmly in place as the club's number one.

After Shilton left in 1992 for Plymouth Argyle, that looked like Taylor's opportunity but just weeks later the Rams moved for the experienced Steve Sutton from Nottingham Forest.

However, Taylor eventually worked his way into the team and blossomed into a goalkeeper of real promise, saving a penalty in the 1993 Anglo-Italian Cup Final at Wembley against Cremonese.

The 1993–94 campaign was his real breakthrough year as he featured in every single League and Cup game, and was named the club's Player of the Year after an outstanding season that ultimately culminated in heartbreak with the Play-off Final defeat to Leicester City.

An agile shot-stopper with good command of his box and the ability to kick effectively with either foot, Taylor was even rumoured to be in line for an England call up before that major setback at Southend.

After his recovery and final appearances for Derby, Taylor joined Wycombe permanently and spent six great years there including playing a major role in their run to the semi-final of the FA Cup in 2001 when they had famously won in the last minute at Leicester in the quarter-final.

He then moved to Barnsley, Telford United and later Burton Albion, where he played his last senior game in August 2004, though he was on the bench for both of the Brewers' FA Cup ties against Manchester United in 2006.

Part of Nigel Clough's coaching team at the Pirelli Stadium, he came back to Derby in 2009 when Clough was appointed manager and, in his first interview with the club's matchday programme, looked back on his career and admitted that the win for Wycombe at Leicester in 2001 was 'payback' for the events of 1994.

Nottingham Forest 2 Derby County 2

16 November 1998

Background

There was not a huge amount of excitement among Derby fans when news first came through that Jim Smith had come out of retirement to take over managing their club

But he took the club straight into the Premier League at the first time of asking and with knowledge of the lower leagues and an eye for a bargain abroad he quickly built up a team that was capable of competing against all but the very best.

By the 1998–99 season the Rams were in their pomp and playing their best top-flight football for many a year.

For Forest, the Brian Clough years were turning into a distant memory. Frank Clark and Stuart Pearce had both had spells in charge and custodianship of the team had passed over to Dave Bassett, a manager who had achieved considerable success with Wimbledon.

The Reds had been relegated from the top-flight at the end of the 1996–97 campaign, but had bounced straight back.

Life at the top was proving a struggle for them. Promotion had been won on the back of the strike partnership of Kevin Campbell and Pierre van Hooijdonk.

Van Hooijdonk claimed that he had been promised team strengthening to make Forest a viable force in the Premier League, but found on his return from the World Cup that Campbell had been sold, Scot Gemmill dropped from the first team after refusing to sign a new contract and club captain Colin Cooper allowed to leave.

The Dutchman took action that was either brave or foolhardy. He went on strike, and remained so until deep into the season. It is fair to say that his return was not particularly welcomed by teammates and supporters alike.

Report

Jim Smith was forced into making changes. Rory Delap was away in Yugoslavia with the Republic of Ireland and Robbie Kozluk was injured so Jacob Laursen played on the right of defence.

Spencer Prior was again available and Stefano Eranio was on the bench as he had been out injured and was not yet fit enough to play a full 90 minutes.

The first half largely belonged to the hosts, although Derby could have taken a first minute lead as Horacio Carbonari nearly managed to give Paulo Wanchope a sniff of goal straight from the kick-off.

Steve Elliott was in early action, first of all taking the ball off the toe of van Hooijdonk before putting in a tackle to deny Steve Stone any attacking opportunities.

Despite the pressure that the Rams were under they did not have too much difficulty in withstanding the onslaught.

Kevin Harper created a good opportunity for Darryl Powell with a break down the right, but Powell chose to head across goal instead of going for the target.

Although Nigel Quashie went close with a strike that flew over the bar the biggest moment of danger came from van Hooijdonk, who placed a 35-yard free-kick perfectly. All that Russell Hoult in the Rams goal could do was to push the ball away for a corner.

Dougie Freedman was righteously indignant not to be awarded a penalty after a clear push in the area by Carbonari.

Derby had similar misfortune earlier when Wanchope played a ball through for Powell who fell over Forest 'keeper Dave Beasant. A penalty would have been harsh though as to the neutral there had been no obvious foul.

If van Hooijdonk was not going to score he was going to make mightily sure that his opponents were not either. Tony Dorigo took a corner from the Derby left and when Carbonari met it with his head there was the Dutchman on the line to clear it.

As the whistle went for the half-time break Wanchope was lying prone in the area, but thankfully he recovered to play in the second half.

Whatever was said at the break saw the tempo of the game increase from the first whistle of the second half.

Harper had suffered a knock late on in the first half and Dean Sturridge, after feeling his way into the game before the break, really started to make a difference to the second period.

There was an element of route one about the visitors' opening goal with a goal-kick from Hoult flicking off Stone and into the path of the speedy Sturridge. The Derby striker muscled his way past Thierry Bonalair. The Frenchman could do little more than upend him for a clear penalty which Dorigo despatched past Beasant coolly.

If the visitors thought that they had broken through, it took less than a minute to convince them that they had not.

Quashie fired in a shot that Hoult could only partly block, allowing Freedman to run the ball over the line and with 57 minutes gone it was 1–1.

There was a certain inevitability that van Hooijdonk would get in on the action after all the nonsense he had caused in the weeks before the game.

Six minutes after going behind Forest were in the lead as the Dutch striker headed home a corner from Scot Gemmill.

The reaction to the goal was incredible. Supporters gave every impression that they would have rather any player in the team score what they hoped would be the winning goal than him, while teammates almost completely ignored him and left van Hooijdonk to celebrate pretty much on his own.

As things transpired it would prove not to be the winner anyway, but before that was the sight that no fan likes to see: a player being stretched off.

On this occasion it was Hoult who had made a brave save at the feet of Stone after Alan Rogers had deceived Carbonari and fired in a wicked cross.

Hoult departed on a stretcher after 69 minutes to be replaced by Mart Poom who was as good a replacement as you could wish for.

Three minutes after the arrival of the Estonian 'keeper between the posts the scoring ended with a goal at the other end.

Dorigo drilled in a cross that Wanchope failed to make full contact with and as the ball squirmed across goal there was Carbonari to fire home and make it 2–2.

There was to be no more scoring but the feeling was that on the day a draw was about the fairest result in the eyes of the neutrals – not that you would find many neutrals in this crowd.

Forest: Beasant, Bonalair, Chettle, Armstrong, Rogers, Stone, Gemmill, Quashie, Bart-Williams, Freedman (Harewood 77), van Hooijdonk.

Subs: Hjelde, Shipperley, Crossley (GK), Gray

Derby: Hoult (Poom 69), Prior, Carbonari, Elliott, Laursen, Bohinen, Powell, Dorigo, Harper (Sturridge 40), Wanchope, Burton.

Subs: Bridge-Wilkinson, Eranio, Baiano

Referee: G. Barber

Booked: Bart-Williams, Rogers, Bonalair (Forest)

Attendance: 24,014

Reaction

Jim Smith was full of praise for the bravery of 'keeper Russell Hoult and said: 'It was a very brave save. It was the ball that caught him rather than Stone's boot – but it came with plenty of force.

'I was satisfied with the way we fought back after going 2–1 down but disappointed that we did not punish them at the end of the game.

'Paulo Wanchope lost a lot of blood following a bang on the nose before half-time. He knows what a local derby is about now and it reminded me of the days when Dave Bassett and I were trying to get out of the lower divisions with Wimbledon and Oxford.

'Horacio took a lot from the Liverpool game. When we rushed him back he played in defeats and began to believe it was his fault. We had to be patient but now he is showing what he can do.

'Jacob Laursen had to play on the right because there were no other options. He'll fit in anywhere if asked and always does a job.

'It was good to see Dean Sturridge so sharp. With the pace we had at the end more might have come from our attacking.'

Forest boss Dave Bassett, a long time friend of Smith, thought that the injury to Hoult was a decisive factor in the outcome of the game.

He added: 'I know it's not an excuse but I think Russell Hoult getting injured and the game stopping for a while didn't help us. Obviously he didn't mean to get injured but we lost our momentum after that.'

What Happened Next

This season represented the high watermark of Jim Smith's reign as Derby manager. The team were playing entertaining and attractive football, and winning important matches as well.

This season saw the first Derby victory at Anfield for many a long year, and later they also beat Liverpool at home for a memorable double.

The week after drawing at Forest the Rams then went down 2–0 at home to West Ham United but they soon picked up their form by winning 1–0 at Southampton with Horacio Carbonari again on target.

That win at The Dell was the first game in a run of just two defeats in 14 in all competitions, including progress in the FA Cup where Derby eventually reached the quarter-final before bowing out in the last minute at Arsenal.

The defeat at Highbury was on the first Saturday in March, and by that point Derby were right in the hunt for European football.

They were also a month away from the return against Forest, the Reds' first visit to Pride Park Stadium.

Featured Player

Horacio Carbonari was one of those rabbits that Jim Smith kept pulling out his hat. A player who nobody had heard of and who was purchased for a reasonable sum, but went on to provide valuable service to Derby County.

With the exception of Paulo Wanchope and his fellow countryman Mauricio Solis, who both came from Costa Rica, all of Smith's foreign imports had come from mainland Europe.

Once Wanchope had broken the mould nowhere seemed off limits for Smith and so it was that Argentinean centre-half Carbonari arrived at Pride Park.

His nickname was Petaco – or bazooka in English – after the thunderbolt shot that he possessed.

At £2.7 million from Rosario Central he was not cheap, but by the time he arrived no player capable of sustaining a career in the top-flight was.

The crowd quickly took to the tall centre-back, and on the occasions that he unleashed it there was little doubt about the ferocity of his shot.

Not all of his nine goals came from spectacular long-range shots as he showed deft control in the opposition box on a number of occasions.

He scored five in his first season at the club with two coming against the old enemy. On the back of his equaliser at the City Ground he would then go on to have an impact on the return game too.

Carbonari fell out of favour at Derby and went on loan to Coventry City, where he played five games in 2002 before calling it a day on his England adventure the following January.

He returned to his first club Rosario Central and played a further 48 games for them, scoring eight times to add to the 26 he had got in his first spell at the club, where he had played 135 times.

Injury truncated his second spell at Rosario and he retired as a player at the end of the 2004–05 season at the age of 31, then later went on to manage the club at the start of the 2006–07 campaign.

Derby County 1 Nottingham Forest 0

10 April 1999

Background

The 1998–99 season was Derby County's third in the Premier League and it marked another year of progress under Jim Smith – so much so that the Rams had their eyes on qualifying for Europe as the campaign approached its business end.

Not since 1976 had Derby faced the challenge of European football having reached the UEFA Cup under Dave Mackay on the back of finishing fourth in Division One the previous season.

They would have done so after finishing fifth in 1989, but for the ban on English clubs because of the Heysel disaster, though this time there were genuine ambitions that Smith could lead his side into the UEFA Cup in what would be only his fourth season in charge.

His first had seen promotion to the Premier League, the second consolidation and the last season at the Baseball Ground, in the third – the first at Pride Park Stadium – the Rams finished ninth, and going in to the April visit of Forest to the club's new home Derby were seventh in the table.

The top four – Manchester United, Arsenal, Chelsea and Leeds United – were out of sight but fifth and sixth were West Ham United and Aston Villa, on 47 and 46 points respectively, while the Rams were a further place back on 44 but with a game in hand over their rivals.

They were even above Liverpool having done the double over the Merseyside giants earlier in what was shaping up to be a potentially rewarding campaign.

Fifth place was the target as that would have guaranteed UEFA Cup football regardless of anything else, though there were other possible scenarios for qualification depending on other matters such as the eventual outcome of the FA Cup.

Smith said ahead of the match: 'There are a couple of possible chinks in the qualifying regulations for Europe but we need points to maintain our position.

'Some of our football in recent home games has been the best we've played all season. We asked them to go for it and be positive but then the problem is marrying the two ends of the pitch.

'In the last two games, we were less solid and defenders have been exposed. We have to get back to collective defending.'

Smith's point was illustrated by Derby's previous outing, a 4–3 defeat at home to Newcastle that swung back and forth, and prior to that they had also shipped four goals away at Leeds United despite taking an early lead.

Darryl Powell had sat out the Newcastle game with a one-match ban but was back for the visit of Forest, something Smith was pleased about, especially having missed out on the deadline-day signing of Seth Johnson from Crewe Alexandra following the sale of Lee Carsley to Blackburn Rovers.

As for Forest, once again they were approaching a trip to Derby at the back end of the season with their relegation almost inevitable – just as they had done in 1997 when heading to the Baseball Ground.

They bounced straight back up in 1998 but after winning two of their first three games they then did not taste three points again until 30 January, and they only added to that ahead of the Derby game with a 13 March victory at Wimbledon.

That all left them bottom, 10 points from safety with only six games remaining and an immediate return to Division One set to arrive sooner rather than later.

'Even though our season may be almost over, the game against Derby County is as important as ever,' admitted goalkeeper Mark Crossley.

'We look at it as a way to salvage some pride. There has not been much for our supporters to smile about this season but, if we beat Derby, they will forget their troubles for a day or two.'

The game also had a bit of extra significance in that it was the first between Derby and Forest at Pride Park Stadium, the Rams' home since the summer of 1997 after their move from the Baseball Ground.

Not that Smith was too fussed about the occasion, the Derby chief revealing: 'I hate local derbies. But they come along all too often and we have to deal with them.

'There is so much local pride involved that there is extra stress on these fixtures.'

Report

In a game that was memorable for its dramatic ending and some controversial moments, sustained periods of quality were lacking.

That was hardly surprising given the visitors' desperation for anything they could get in their bid to avoid relegation, while Derby struggled to impose their superiority on proceedings as they chased European football.

The first half was notable mainly for one incident with 16 minutes on the clock when Vassilis Borbokis appeared to take an elbow from Pierre van Hooijdonk and, after collapsing again having attempted to get up following treatment, left the field on a stretcher.

Derby fans called for a red card but the referee did not even call for a foul, nor did he stop play when the Rams' recent signing from Sheffield United was down injured, instead waiting for the ball to go out before he called for medical assistance.

Borbokis's replacement, Dean Sturridge, then proved Derby's biggest attacking threat and was twice spectacularly denied in the first half by Mark Crossley.

Derby were largely in control though they also had an escape before the break when Marlon Harewood rounded Russell Hoult but his shot lacked power and Horacio Carbonari cleared off the line.

That would not be Carbonari's last major incident in the match but as the second period progressed, Hoult was sent off for catching Forest's Alan Rogers with a foul outside the penalty box.

Forest had their moments with more men on the field but 10 minutes after Hoult's departure, Richard Gough collected his second yellow card and also followed for an early bath.

Five minutes from time came Carbonari's second goal against Forest in his debut season at Pride Park, though what he was doing so far up the field with the game on a knife-edge at 0–0, nobody knew.

He advanced forward unnoticed by the visitors and picked up Lars Bohinen's pass outside the penalty area.

There was still work to do but he beat Steve Chettle and Christian Edwards with ease before, showing the composure of a top-quality striker, planting an excellent shot past Crossley and into the corner.

It was a moment of high quality not in keeping with the game overall – but it was enough to earn Derby's first League win over Forest since November 1990.

Derby: Hoult, Prior, Carbonari, Laursen, Schnoor, Borbokis (Sturridge 16), Bohinen, Powell, Baiano (Harper HT), Burton (Poom 59), Wanchope.

Other Subs: Dorigo, Elliott

Forest: Crossley, Louis-Jean, Gough, Edwards, Bonalair, Freedman, Johnson, Palmer, Rogers, van Hooijdonk (Shipperley 76), Harewood (Chettle 79).

Other Subs: Woan, Allou, Goodlad (GK)

Referee: G. Barber

Booked: Johnson, Rogers, Edwards, Harewood, Gough (Forest)

Sent off: Hoult (Derby); Gough (Forest)

Attendance: 32,217

Reaction

Two red cards, a player carried off on a stretcher early in the first half after a nasty clash, and a late winning goal from a centre-half that would not have looked out of place scored by a world-class striker – there were certainly plenty of talking points from this match.

The highlight for Rams fans was, of course, Horacio Carbonari's sublime goal five minutes from time to give his side the three points.

Carbonari, Derby's record signing, backed up his equaliser at the City Ground in November with the winner at Pride Park in April to make sure that whatever else he did while with the Rams, he would always be remembered for what he did against Forest.

'It was a great goal,' said Derby manager Jim Smith. 'Once he got himself into that position, I backed him to score because he is very confident in front of goal.

'He has the ability to score goals like that. Horacio is a long way from his home in Argentina and he has been getting to know the style. I believe we will see the very best from him next season but he produced the moment of great skill in a poor game.'

The other major issue arising from the game was a season-ending injury for Vassilis Borbokis, the Greek defender who fractured his cheekbone after a clash with Pierre van Hooijdonk.

It was clear immediately that Borbokis, in only his fourth game for the Rams, was seriously injured, although referee Graham Barber declined to award a free-kick having been in a great position.

Replays later suggested that van Hooijdonk deliberately swung his elbow in Borbokis's direction, although it appeared that the footage did the Dutchman no favours and the incident was generally accepted as an accident.

'I thought it was Vass's momentum as much as the elbow that caused the damage,' said Smith. 'When you see it on video it does not look better but my impression was that it was not a deliberate elbow.'

Forest manager Ron Atkinson added: 'I'm not trying to defend Pierre if he did wrong but the referee was very close and had the best view in the place. And he is not one who is reluctant to book people.'

Both sides were reduced to 10 men in the second half with Derby goalkeeper Russell Hoult seeing red for a professional foul, while Forest's Richard Gough walked for two bookings, though both dismissals were also deemed harsh.

The win saw Derby keep up their challenge for European football while it also left Forest rooted to the foot of the table and meant their already slim chances of avoiding the drop had become even more remote.

Atkinson said: 'Our quality is not as good as it should be but in almost every game there has been a good spirit among the lads.

'I did not think there was any malice or violence in Richard Gough's two fouls but I find a centre-half waltzing round two defenders before scoring harder to take than bookings or a sending-off.'

What Happened Next

The Rams were more than in the running for a place in the following season's UEFA Cup after beating Forest but things soon started to turn sour.

A week later they crashed 5–1 at West Ham United, one of the other sides challenging for a European place, and the only plus point to come from the defeat was a promising debut as a substitute for 17-year-old midfielder Adam Murray.

A drab 0–0 draw at home to Southampton followed, then came a 1–0 defeat at Arsenal which saw striker Marvin Robinson become the second youth product to make his debut in a couple of weeks, before the Rams got back to winning ways by beating Leicester City 2–1 at Filbert Street.

Pride Park's season came to a close with another goalless draw, this time against Coventry City, then 1998–99 was ended with a 2–1 defeat at Chelsea that left Derby eighth after their form tailed away in the last few weeks.

It was, however, their highest finish since they ended the 1988–89 season fifth in the old First Division under Arthur Cox.

The famous photograph of Nottingham Forest's players with the FA Cup in 1898 —wearing Derby County's kit!

Picture courtesy of Nottingham Forest

Derby's Gerry Daly takes on former Ram Archie Gemmill in a clash between the rivals at the City Ground.

Picture by the *Derby Telegraph*

Kevin Harper holds off Forest's Chris Bart-Williams in the November 1998 draw at the City Ground.

Picture by the *Derby Telegraph*

The Rams celebrate Horacio Carbonari's winner against Forest at Pride Park in 1999.

Celebrations start after Paul Peschisolido makes it 3–0 to Derby having earlier scored the 'coffee cup goal' in March 2004.

Morten Bisgaard starts the move that led to Derby's first goal in the December 2004 victory at Pride Park. Picture by the *Derby Telegraph*

A rarity — Forest legend Stuart Pearce captaining Derby and kissing the badge after scoring! This was in the benefit game for Ted McMinn against Rangers in 2006.

Picture by Andy Clarke

Pesch returned to Pride Park in the build-up to the November 2008 fixture to recreate his moment with the coffee cup!

Tito Villa celebrates his equaliser in November 2008 — having earlier scored an own-goal to put Forest in front.
Picture by Andy Clarke

Miles Addison's late header was controversially chalked-off in the November 2008 draw.
Picture by Andy Clarke

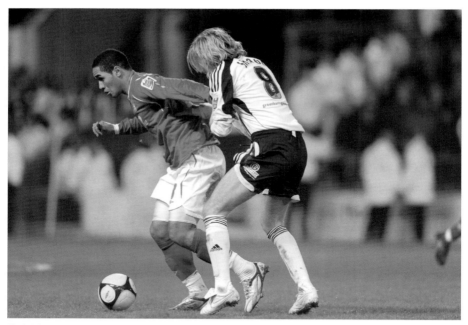

Robbie Savage gets to grips with Lewis McGugan in the FA Cup comeback of February 2009.
Picture by Andy Clarke

Kris Commons fires in the memorable City Ground winner against his old club.
Picture by Andy Clarke

The Rams rush to Kris Commons after his FA Cup cracker at the City Ground.

Picture by Andy Clarke

Lewin Nyatanga celebrates the opening goal in the February 2009 Championship win at Forest.

Picture by Andy Clarke

More scarf-waving by Robbie Savage after victory at the City Ground.

Rams fans cheer their team on at the City Ground.   Pictures by Andy Clarke

Miles Addison heads the ball clear during the August 2009 defeat at Forest.
Picture by Andy Clarke

Jeff Hendrick strokes in his goal at the City Ground in September 2011.

Picture by Andy Clarke

Hendrick wheels away to the Derby support in celebration.

Picture by Andy Clarke

Theo Robinson is quick to congratulate Jeff Hendrick on what proved to be the crucial goal in a remarkable City Ground victory.   Picture by Andy Clarke

Nathan Tyson moved from Forest to Derby in the summer of 2011 — then made his Rams debut at the City Ground.

Picture by Andy Clarke

The Rams celebrate with the Brian Clough Trophy after their thrilling win at Forest with only 10 men.

Picture by Andy Clarke

They were overtaken by Liverpool, while West Ham finished fifth and reached the UEFA Cup after progressing through the Intertoto Cup.

Defeat for Forest only served to accelerate their relegation from the Premier League and after they lost their next two fixtures, at home to Tottenham Hotspur then away to Aston Villa, it was all over.

At least Forest did manage to salvage some pride with victories in their final three fixtures, including at Blackburn Rovers which relegated their hosts too, but it had been a terrible season for the team from the City Ground and they finished bottom, 11 points from safety.

Featured Player

Russell Hoult might want to forget his two appearances for Derby against Nottingham Forest in 1998–99 – because he started both but did not manage to complete either game!

The goalkeeper had been firmly established as Derby's number one during his first two full seasons with the club but in 1997–98 he played second-fiddle to Mart Poom and made only two Premier League appearances that campaign.

However, manager Jim Smith opted for Hoult over Poom at the start of 1998–99 and the Englishman deservedly kept his place with some excellent displays and was in good form by the time the November visit to Nottingham Forest came around.

On a dramatic night at the City Ground, Hoult only made it as far as 69 minutes when he was carried off on a stretcher after a nasty collision while making a save to bring an early end to his night.

Hoult was not back in the team until January, when Poom picked up an injury, but even when the Estonian returned a month later it was Hoult who kept his place.

The return against Forest in April saw him again start but not finish – and this time he only lasted for 59 minutes before he was sent off for a professional foul on the Reds' Alan Rogers outside the penalty area.

He made one more appearance that season, before his suspension started, and that was it for the campaign, though more injury problems for Poom saw Hoult featuring regularly in the early months of 1999–2000.

That was, however, until an error in a 2–0 defeat at Liverpool in November 1999, coupled with the return of Poom, cost Hoult his place – and ultimately his Derby career.

The game at Anfield proved his last in a Derby shirt and he joined Portsmouth the following January, initially on loan before completing a permanent deal.

Signed from Leicester in 1995, Hoult was an extremely able goalkeeper during his time with Derby and at the peak of his performances was even being talked about for a possible England call up.

He made 138 appearances for the Rams before joining Pompey, and he was again in excellent form with West Bromwich Albion to keep record-breaking numbers of clean sheets and once more be talked about for England.

Hoult had a loan spell with Nottingham Forest in 2005 – one of 12 English clubs he has appeared for, including all four major East Midlands clubs as he later lined up with Notts County.

It seemed his playing career was over when he joined Hereford United as goalkeeping coach in 2010 but, after becoming assistant manager the following year, he made two emergency appearances for the Bulls at the start of 2011–12.

Derby County 4 Nottingham Forest 2

20 March 2004

Background

Make no mistake, Derby County were in big trouble as they prepared to welcome Nottingham Forest to Pride Park Stadium in March 2004.

The Rams had been struggling at the wrong end of the table all season and a 2–1 defeat away to Watford the Tuesday before this encounter had left them in the bottom three of the First Division, two points away from safety with only 10 games remaining.

But George Burley's men were certainly able to take consolation from their home form having gone six without defeat in front of their own supporters and had not been breached on home soil so far in 2004.

And they also had something of a potential ace up their sleeve in the shape of experienced striker Paul Peschisolido.

The Canadian had arrived after a 0–0 draw at home to Crewe Alexandra, in which the Rams laid siege to the visitors' goal but could not break through, and then he marked his debut with the only strike in a 1–0 win over Rotherham United.

Pesch was also on the mark in that defeat at Watford and was already looking like a shrewd acquisition by Burley.

But most of the build-up in the Derby camp surrounded giant teenager Tom Huddlestone, not so much of a man-mountain as a boy-mountain having cemented his place in the team at the age of 16 right at the start of the season.

Huddlestone, 17 by the time the game arrived, was born in Nottingham and was with Forest as a very young player before moving to Derby at Under-13 level.

But there would be no split loyalties for him and he admitted: 'I supported Chelsea as a youngster and although most of my family support Forest they are just happy to see me do well and I think they would rather us get three points than Forest on Saturday.

'Some of my mates are Forest fans and they give me stick sometimes, but I hope to keep them quiet on Saturday.

'The atmosphere at the City Ground back in September (the game finished 1–1 with Junior on target for Derby) was good and hopefully we'll be able to better that at Pride Park.'

Huddlestone was not the only Nottingham lad in Derby's team with experienced defender Michael Johnson having been born and grown up just a few miles along the A52 – and he was also a self-confessed lifelong Forest fan.

And the former Jamaica international explained: 'I was born and raised in Nottingham and spent a lot of time as a kid following Forest and the local derby games.

'I know some Rams say they could cope with relegation so long as we beat Forest. I can't quite believe that's true, but I do know how much this game means.'

Forest went in to the game in slightly better shape than Derby, although not by much, as they sat 17th in the table and four points better off than their hosts.

They had been boosted by a recent run of just one defeat in their last eight games and travelled to Pride Park having taken four points from two successive home fixtures, the second a 1–1 draw at home to Burnley some 24 hours after the Rams had lost at Watford.

Having reached the Play-off semi-finals the previous season, Forest had struggled to replicate that form in 2003–04 and with Joe Kinnear in charge they were languishing in the lower part of the bottom half.

But with the season edging towards its final stages they had not been sucked right in to the relegation battle and Kinnear was confident that his side would have enough to avoid trouble.

He felt the pressure was all on the Rams and, having only been in charge of Forest for a little over a month, he was looking forward to his first East Midlands derby occasion.

Leading in to the game, he said: 'We've got everything to play for and I'm sure it will be a fantastic occasion. I'm looking forward to it because I haven't been to a game between the two clubs before.

'I must admit I don't know too much about games between Forest and Derby. I've been told that it's the only game that matters to both sets of supporters because of the rivalry that exists between the two clubs.

'They tell me the atmosphere is good and I'm sure all the players are looking forward to it.

'Games between Forest and Derby have been very tight over the last couple of years but bring it on. Let's go for it! We will go there well prepared and although I wouldn't say that confidence is sky high, it's certainly very good.'

Report

Any victory for Derby over their local rivals is always going to have its talking points but the one incident everyone wanted to discuss after this match was what became known as the 'coffee cup goal'.

Derby were already a goal up when Forest 'keeper Barry Roche lined up a first-time clearance from a back-pass in what looked to be a harmless 28th-minute situation.

But with strong winds swirling around Pride Park Stadium, a coffee cup had been blown on to the pitch and could not have been positioned any better as it lay in wait before deflecting the ball slightly off course, leading Roche to spoon his clearance into the path of Paul Peschisolido for a simple tap-in to an unguarded net.

Replays showed the lid coming off the cup and coffee spilling on to the pitch, adding even more of an element of comedy to the moment.

Derby had opened the scoring in the fourth minute through a crisp finish from skipper Ian Taylor, and by the time Peschisolido had made it three by tucking home Marcus Tudgay's pass on 37 it looked like the game was all over.

Forest had other ideas and were back in the game just before half-time through Gareth Taylor's bundled effort, then on 68 minutes they really set Derby's nerves jangling with a second from Gareth Williams.

However, rather than try to hang on, George Burley switched the emphasis from defence to attack and he was rewarded nine minutes from time when Tudgay hammered home a fourth goal from the edge of the box.

It had been an exciting encounter but one moment would live longer in the memory than anything else.

Derby: Grant, Kenna, Jackson (Boertien HT), M. Johnson, Mawene, I. Taylor, Huddlestone, Costa (Holmes 71), Osman, Peschisolido, Tudgay.

Other Subs: Oakes (GK), Tome, Whelan

Forest: Roche, Louis-Jean, Dawson, Impey, Morgan, Williams, Jess, Barmby (D. Johnson 33), G. Taylor, Sonner, Reid.

Other Subs: Formann (GK), Thompson, Doig, Westcarr

Referee: D. Pugh

Booked: Dawson, Reid, Williams, Taylor (Forest)

Attendance: 32,390

Reaction

While the match went down as a massive win for the Rams in terms of helping them hold on to their First Division status, it also went down as the day the 'coffee cup goal' was scored.

Rarely has there been a goal in such bizarre circumstances anywhere in football, let alone in the annals of Derby County's history, but for anyone in black and white it immediately became a legendary moment.

Paul Peschisolido was the grateful recipient of one of the more unlikely assists you will ever see and his understated celebration summed up the sheer bewilderment of what had just happened.

'I felt really sorry for the 'keeper,' he admitted afterwards. 'It must have bobbled up as he hit it and he shinned it to me. I turned, expecting him to have the ball, and there it was in front of me so I stuck it in the net.'

The brace took Pesch's tally to four goals in just three games since he joined Derby from Sheffield United, and he added: 'I was pleased to have a part in the goals and to have scored two.

'We know what a win over Forest means to the supporters and we wanted to go out and do our best for them. We are in a situation where we need to win every game so today was useful.'

While Pesch netted twice and shared the headlines with a certain coffee cup, it was skipper Ian Taylor who had started the afternoon off with a fine finish after just four minutes.

The former Aston Villa man had arrived at Derby the previous summer and was already a firm favourite among the home fans well before netting against the club's big rivals.

And of a quite remarkable day, Taylor admitted: 'I'm feeling a mixture of frustration and elation really. We played really well – but why can't we do that every week?

'The conditions were awful. It was really windy but I think we adapted better than they did. We tried to stick the ball in behind them for most of the game and it worked for us.

'I just gambled on the ball though and with the wind helping by holding it up I was through on goal. I just took my time and whacked it!'

Reaction coming out of the visiting dressing room was somewhat quieter after what was a pretty poor performance by Forest and certainly a defeat they did not want to suffer – let alone under the circumstances of the 90 minutes.

The result had dragged Forest to just a point outside of the relegation zone, although boss Joe Kinnear stuck steadfastly to his belief that his side had more than enough in their locker to get out of trouble.

And he later admitted: 'Quite simply, we were awful in so many respects of the game at Derby.'

What Happened Next

Although it was a big result for Derby they failed to build on it immediately and picked up just two points from their next four games, a little run that also saw them go down 1–0 at home to relegation rivals Walsall and suffer their first Pride Park reverse of 2004.

By that point they really were in serious danger as they remained in the bottom three while the teams above them had games in hand.

But the last game of their four without a win was a solid 0–0 draw at West Ham United then in successive home fixtures they beat fellow strugglers Bradford City in a 3–2 thriller and thumped Preston North End 5–1 with a resounding display.

The Preston win lifted Derby up to 19th and the finish line was in sight but a 1–0 defeat at Burnley – also in deep trouble themselves – ended April on a negative note.

Safety was, however, still in their own hands, and after Walsall had lost their penultimate game on the afternoon of 1 May Derby were able to confirm their survival in the evening by beating FA Cup finalists Millwall 2–0 at Pride Park Stadium, sparking emotional scenes more based on relief than celebration.

Derby eventually stayed up by a single point in what was George Burley's first full season in charge, but the Scot masterminded a tremendous turnaround in his second by taking the Rams from fifth-bottom to fourth from top.

Off the field they certainly milked the victory for as much as they could get out of it by bringing out the game on video and DVD, including all the build-up and reaction, entitling it *Gone With the Wind*.

As for the cup itself, that was retrieved by a member of the club's staff and was signed by Paul Peschisolido before being put on display at the stadium!

The result certainly galvanised Forest and actually proved to be their last defeat of the season.

They finished strongly and went undefeated in their last eight, a run that hauled them up to 14th in the table and saw them ultimately end up eight points clear of Derby.

Featured Player

Paul Peschisolido was already fast becoming a Derby County favourite but cemented that status with two goals to see off rivals Nottingham Forest on 20 March 2004.

And they were contrasting strikes too – the first simply sheer opportunism after Forest 'keeper Barry Roche's clearance had spooned up the Canadian's way after the intervention of the famous coffee cup, the second a clinical finish after a quick one-two with Marcus Tudgay.

That took Pesch's tally to four in three games and showed just why George Burley had been so keen to bring him to Derby from Sheffield United a couple of weeks previously.

Sensing the need for extra experience in his striking ranks, Burley swooped for Pesch and was immediately repaid.

Pesch was 33 when he joined the Rams and showed all of the predatory instincts he had displayed over a long career spread across seven clubs prior to his arrival at Pride Park Stadium.

He previously had history against Forest from his days at Sheffield United, netting a spectacular extra-time strike in their 2003 Play-off semi-final second leg at Bramall Lane before whipping off his shirt in celebration and mouthing the words 'oh my God!' over and over.

Pesch added nine goals in 2004–05 as the Rams finished fourth, and he started both of the season's games against Forest without scoring.

Having scored Derby's final goal under Burley he then netted the opening one under Phil Brown on the first day of 2005–06 but as the season wore on he became more of an impact player off the bench, scoring his last goal of a difficult campaign in January.

Pesch's last season with Derby saw him net four times, all from the bench, although his popularity among fans never wavered and neither did his commitment to the cause, and he was given a start in his last game for the club – the 2007 Play-off Final victory over West Bromwich Albion at Wembley.

He left the club that summer having made 47 starts, a further 56 appearances as a substitute, and in that time he scored 24 goals.

After ending his playing career with Luton Town, Pesch became assistant manager at St Patrick's Athletic with his former Derby teammate Jeff Kenna before, in the summer of 2009, taking over as boss of Burton Albion following the Brewers' promotion to the Football League.

He lost his job at Burton in March 2012.

Derby County 3 Nottingham Forest 0

11 December 2004

Background

George Burley had been brought to Derby initially as a short-term measure in the spring of 2003 to prevent things unravelling entirely after relegation from the Premier League and the John Gregory period appeared to be leading the club to disaster.

Gregory had been in charge for 55 matches when the board called time on his spell in charge. He was not sacked but suspended over allegations of some form of misconduct. What he was supposed to have done was never publicly revealed and charges were eventually dropped and Gregory was compensated.

For one match Mark Lillis, who had coached under Gregory, was placed in charge, but at that time the club needed someone with experience to keep matters on an even keel.

Burley was originally given the title of 'interim manager', but proved so successful in stopping the rot that he was given the job on a permanent footing during the summer.

The 2003-04 season proved a difficult one for Derby once more as they continued to fight against relegation but with Burley at the helm they were always in with more than a shout of staying up.

That they did owed much to Burley's tactical awareness and some shrewd signings at important times, plus a few key victories – including one over Forest that is covered elsewhere in this book.

During 2003–04 the club was taken over by a consortium and it was under the new regime that Derby were able to move smartly in the transfer market in the summer of 2004 to bring in the likes of Tommy Smith, Inigo Idiakez and Morten Bisgaard.

Burley had an astute eye for a bargain with players picked up from the English leagues as well as total unknowns from abroad who were seamlessly moulded into an entertaining and attractive side that knew how to win in style.

But given the summer to start building a side it took a while for the Rams to hit their stride – they lost all but two of their opening seven matches in all competitions, including a League Cup exit at League Two side Lincoln City.

By the time that Forest came round in December they had won eight Championship fixtures, and after their slow start they had stabilised a little by only losing four times across September, October and November.

The week prior to welcoming their rivals, the Rams had scored twice right at the death to earn a 2–2 draw at home to Coventry City – the fourth time already in the season they had overturned a two-goal deficit although one of those occasions, at home to Crewe Alexandra, had ended ultimately in defeat.

One of the goals against Coventry had been scored by Polish international striker Grzegorz Rasiak, who had joined the Rams in September after a long and patient chase that was rewarded with the tall front man quickly becoming a favourite at Pride Park.

Going into this match Derby were 10th in the table, while Forest sat in the relegation zone in 22nd place with 20 points and were without a win since the middle of November.

Apart from Rotherham United, who were bottom with 11 points, there were only 13 points separating second-from-bottom Gillingham and eighth-placed Leicester City, all going to show how tight the division was.

The Rams were 10 points off relegation and 11 off automatic promotion.

Report

George Burley made a couple of changes from the side that had come back to earn a draw against Coventry in the previous game.

Ian Taylor started in place of Marco Reich as the team was given a more solid midfield, and Paul Peschisolido, who had come off the bench in the Coventry match, kept his place in the starting line-up as Burley opted for a little and large strike partnership of Pesch and Grzegorz Rasiak.

Michael Johnson passed a fitness test and Derby went with a defence featuring Richard Jackson and Jeff Kenna at full-back, with a Nottingham-born pairing at centre-half of Johnson and Tom Huddlestone.

Conditions on the day were as good as possible and the Rams were almost ahead within the first minute. Rasiak and Peschisolido combined but fortunately for the visitors Andy Impey was up to the task and cleared.

These fixtures have a history of early goals falling to one team or the other, so it was little surprise that Derby found themselves a goal ahead before Forest had even had time to gather their thoughts.

The free-flowing nature of a Rams side whose every move was strictly orchestrated by Spanish midfield general Inigo Idiakez was perfectly illustrated in just the third minute.

The first goal came after a combination of Taylor, Jeff Kenna, and Morten Bisgaard left the Forest defence chasing shadows as their slick inter passing tore the visitors apart.

Bisgaard found Idiakez, who had the simple task of laying the ball into the path of Tommy Smith for a neat and composed finish beyond Paul Gerrard and into the back of the net.

As with most local derby matches this was a full-blooded affair with both sides determined to take the upper-hand.

Wes Morgan headed over from a corner before Rasiak had an opportunity that he wasted by dallying too long on the edge of the box, then Bisgaard tried to fashion an opening but despite his tricky footwork Morgan managed to cut out his cross.

There was an obvious difference in styles between the two teams with Forest aiming for target man Gareth Taylor at every opportunity while Derby utilised a more cultured passing game.

Derby should have doubled their lead in the 20th minute. Paul Evans hauled Bisgaard down and conceded a free-kick, from which Taylor saw his header handled by Impey and referee Graham Laws had little problem in awarding a penalty.

The referee felt that a penalty and yellow card were sufficient punishment, and then he followed up by booking Gerrard for time-wasting.

Only Taylor would know if all the delays distracted him but the end result that his spot kick ended up flying over the bar rather than nestling in the back of the net suggested that it did.

The miss drained some of the belief from the home side, and the Reds fed on that. David Johnson and Impey both worked their way into dangerous positions but the Derby defence survived.

Burley's men tried to build up their momentum once more, and started to create half chances as the game wore on. The visitors were beginning to get frustrated as could be clearly seen by an exchange between coach Mick Harford on the sidelines and an isolated Andy Reid who was seeing little of the action from the left wing.

It took Joe Kinnear's side until the 39th minute to fashion their best chance of the half. Jack Lester and Evans drew the Derby defence into giving away a foul in a dangerous position: the penalty area D.

At last Andy Reid had a chance to shine and his curling free-kick beat Lee Camp in the Derby goal all ends up but thankfully for the Rams flew narrowly wide of the upright.

Peschisolido tried to win himself a penalty after a push by Alan Rogers but was booked for diving for his trouble, and with the watch ticking down to the break a throw by Kenna was almost converted by Rasiak as he spun on the ball and could only watch as Gerrard managed to keep it out of the goal.

Four minutes were added to the end of the first half as the game started to get tasty with Gareth Taylor's seemingly cynical chop on young Huddlestone not even meriting a yellow card in the eyes of the referee.

While the Rams used the full 15 minutes of half-time to sort out any problems and fire themselves up for the second 45, Forest were out early to renew battle.

Although it had been a full-blooded contest both teams lined up for the kick-off with the same players that had fought out the first half.

For Lester though the game was over after 49 minutes when he fell awkwardly after tangling with Smith. The striker was stretchered off to be replaced by John Thompson.

Testosterone seemed to be flying all over the place with first David and Michael Johnson squaring up to each other and then Idiakez and Gareth Taylor doing the same.

The theme continued as Michael Dawson fouled Peschisolido and then earned more annoyance from the Derby crowd as he hooked a goalbound ball away from under the crossbar.

With less than 30 minutes remaining Kinnear felt that there was still a game there to be won and brought on a third forward in Marlon King in place of midfielder Adam Nowland.

As a sign of the nature of the game Idiakez was booked after 73 minutes, and thus became the seventh name in the referee's notebook, but the game was effectively over with 15 minutes remaining as the silkier skills of the hosts once more made Forest pay.

Neat inter-passing left Smith free on the left. He beat Thompson before cutting inside and firing a cross to the far post where Rasiak headed home and made it a comfortable 2–0 to the Rams.

Forest were not going to give up without a fight and twice went close as first Thompson had a shot tipped over and then Gareth Taylor headed narrowly wide.

Both managers continued making substitutions as the game wore on, but it was Derby who continued to hold the upper hand.

The third and final goal came with only three minutes of regulation time remaining. Idiakez started it but when he lost possession Taylor was there to take over.

Taylor found Bisgaard who launched a first-time ball across the box. Rasiak read his intentions perfectly and arrived at the right moment to fire home his second and Derby's third of the match.

Adam Bolder, on as a late substitute, nearly added a fourth during the four minutes of stoppage-time, but it did not matter as the Rams had recorded their biggest victory over the old enemy since November 1979.

Derby: Camp, Kenna, I. Taylor, Bisgaard, M. Johnson (Mills 90), Peschisolido (Reich 86), Smith, Jackson, Huddlestone, Rasiak, Idiakez (Bolder 90).

Subs: Grant (GK), Tudgay

Forest: Gerrard, Impey, Rogers, Nowland (King 63), Morgan, Dawson, Reid, Evans, D. Johnson (Robertson 74), G. Taylor, Lester (Thompson 49).

Subs: Doyle (GK), Hjelde

Referee: G. Laws

Booked: Kenna, Johnson, Idiakez, Peschisolido (Derby); Gerrard, Impey, Reid, Evans, Taylor (Forest)

Attendance: 30,793

Reaction

George Burley was unsurprisingly delighted at victory over Derby's local rivals, a second in the year, and admitted after the game: 'I think we have shown the fans this season that we have come a long way and today we were on top from start to finish.

'I'm pleased for the fans because it's been a difficult few years. Because we hadn't won any of our previous three games I think there was a bit of tension, but we came through.

'You couldn't single anyone out. Going forward we were outstanding and everyone played a part today.

'You don't mind how you score but today we hit three very good goals – the build-up play was outstanding. The penalty miss could have knocked us back but we came back well in the second half.'

What Happened Next

By the time the two teams met for this game their respective seasons were pretty much taking shape, and what happened over the following months only served to re-emphasise that fact.

The victory was Derby's first of three on the spin, including wins at Plymouth Argyle and promotion-chasing Wigan Athletic, and they continued to collect points in January and February to put themselves among the Play-off candidates.

The return game at the City Ground late in February saw Grzegorz Rasiak again score twice but this time it finished 2–2, though by that point while the Rams were looking upwards Forest were in big trouble.

Forest actually collected more points than Derby in March, due to a quirk in the fixture list leaving the Rams with just three games, though in April the future became clearer for both clubs.

Four successive wins kept Derby in Play-off contention while Forest's form deserted them and they were finally relegated on the penultimate weekend of the season, while the Rams confirmed fourth spot by beating Preston North End on the last day.

That earned them a two-legged semi-final against Preston, who were managed by Billy Davies – later to have influential spells at both East Midlands clubs.

A 2–0 defeat in the away leg and a 0–0 draw back at home saw the Rams season end with them still in the Championship, but after the misery of relegation from the top-flight three years previously and further struggles in this division the campaign had to go down as a successful one with more highs than lows.

Forest's failure to claw themselves away from the relegation zone began a three-year spell in League One for them that saw a temporary halt to games between the two clubs at opposite ends of Brian Clough Way.

Featured Player

There was a lot of controversy over the period that the group known as the Three Amigos were in charge, and especially of the role played by Murdo Mackay who was the only member of the board with any real football knowledge having worked as an agent in Scotland.

It was Mackay who brought the unknown Grzegorz Rasiak to the club after he discovered that the Pole had been signed by Italian club AC Sienna but was unable to play for them as they had exceeded their quota of foreign players.

Derby signed Rasiak and he was a revelation. He played 41 times for the Rams and hit the back of the net on 18 occasions.

Two goals in a victory against Forest would have guaranteed him popularity among fans, but he added to that with two more in the 2–2 draw at the City Ground as part of a contribution to a season that saw the Rams facing the end-of-season Play-offs rather than the regular battle against relegation.

As with so much that occurred under the Three Amigos regime, Rasiak's time at Derby ended in controversy.

By August 2005 Phil Brown was manager and he could only react in horror when the board told him that his striker had been sold to Tottenham Hotspur during the final hours of the summer transfer window.

The hour of closure for the window was different in the Premier League and the Football League. The League's offices closed at 5pm while Premier League business continued deep into the evening.

Rams fans watched their window shut with relief believing that their squad was intact only to find out that their striker had in fact gone.

Equally as bad for Brown as the news a player had been sold from under his nose was the knowledge that even if he was allowed a percentage of the money from Rasiak, there was no way he could spend it as business was now closed for his division.

Rasiak failed to score for Spurs and moved on. He similarly failed to net a solitary goal for Bolton Wanderers in a brief spell there but continued to be a scourge for Championship defences with Southampton, Watford and Reading, suggesting that this was his true level.

None of which bothered Derby fans who only knew that they had lost a striker with more than enough quality for them.

Derby County 1 Nottingham Forest 1

2 November 2008

Background

The contrasting fortunes of the two teams over the previous few seasons meant that more than three years had passed since Derby County and Nottingham Forest last met in a competitive fixture.

Forest's relegation to League One at the end of 2004–05 came in a campaign that saw Derby reach the Play-off semi-final, and two years later the Play-offs put the clubs two divisions apart as the Rams went up to the Premier League after winning at Wembley while the Reds failed in their bid to escape the third tier at the last-four stage.

But the 2007–08 campaign proved a leveller as Derby's visit to the promised land of the top-flight quickly turned into a nightmare with the ultimate humiliation of suffering relegation earlier than any team had previously done so and breaking a whole host of unwanted records along the way, notably setting the Premier League's lowest-ever points total of 11.

In contrast, along the A52, the 2007–08 season went down as the one that finally saw Forest, the first team to fall to their country's third tier having earlier won the European Cup, finally make their mark on League One – although it took them until the final day of the campaign to do so.

Both clubs went to work over the summer with Derby, under Paul Jewell, making wholesale changes to their squad, while Forest were also active in the transfer market.

Notably, the great rivals raided each other – a rare occurrence in itself, let alone one player heading in each direction of what was by now known as Brian Clough Way.

The most controversial of the moves was that of Kris Commons, who scored one of the goals to help Forest to promotion on the final day.

The winger's contract was due to expire at the end of the campaign and despite the Reds' attempts to keep him on, Commons rejected their approaches to the degree that he was actually released by the club shortly after promotion was secured.

It was soon confirmed that he was in talks over a move to Derby and he quickly put pen to paper, becoming the first player to join Derby from Forest in 15 years – a big move for a self-confessed Forest fan.

Not that Forest were any less guilty of looking down the road for a big summer deal as they raided Pride Park Stadium for Derby's record signing Robert Earnshaw, who had joined the club the previous summer for £3.5 million from Norwich City but a return of just two goals showed that he failed to live up to his billing.

It was not a surprise to see Earnshaw depart Derby, though his move to Forest perhaps was, given the rarity of transfers between the two clubs.

Although Earnshaw was their only signing from Derby, Forest did not stop there with an autumn move for goalkeeper Lee Camp from Queens Park Rangers.

Camp, Derby born and bred, was – like Commons – widely known to be a supporter of his home club and had come through the Rams' ranks to make himself an England Under-21 international.

Given all of that, the 2 November 2008 match could not come around soon enough once the fixtures had been revealed, and it was not a shock to see Sky Sports soon select it for live broadcast.

Derby actually went in to the game in pretty decent form with just one defeat since the end of August, a run of 10 games, and they had warmed up nicely with a 3–1 win at home to Norwich City the previous Tuesday night that left them 10th in the table with their year-long wait for a victory well and truly behind them.

Forest had also prepared for the game with a midweek success, 2–1 away at Crystal Palace, although that was just a small consolation to their supporters as it was only their second of the campaign and the first since August, the sequence of results ensuring they travelled to Pride Park second from bottom in the Championship.

The build-up was dominated by talk of Commons, Camp and Earnshaw coming up against their former clubs, although Derby boss Jewell was keen to focus on the overall occasion.

In previewing the game he said: 'I have played in derby games before but this is what you would call a proper derby. Both clubs are good-sized clubs and this game has got all of the makings of a tasty encounter.

'I was born in Liverpool and I would say that this game compares with the Liverpool-Everton game. Every derby game has its pride at stake and the Forest game is that one for us. For our supporters it is huge, as it is for Forest, and there is an intense rivalry.'

There were similar noises coming out of the City Ground, with manager Colin Calderwood admitting: 'It's something I've looked forward to and I know it's a priority for the fans.

'Almost since the day we got promotion until the fixtures came out, it was one I was desperate to be involved in and sample the atmosphere. I want to enjoy it and that's what we intend to do.'

Report

It is fair to say that stoppage-time was about as dramatic and controversial as it gets, particularly given the circumstances of a local derby encounter.

With the board having gone up to signal time added on, the score was level at 1–1 leaving Forest looking set for a point despite having had Lewis McGugan sent off in the 74th minute.

Then Derby looked to have nicked the win when Miles Addison powered a header home – only for referee Stuart Attwell to blow for a penalty, while Addison was heading the ball, after Luke Chambers handled.

Lee Camp turned Nacer Barazite's spot-kick around the post then from the resulting corner he pushed a Przemyslaw Kazmierczak header wide.

That meant another flag-kick which Addison again met with another fine header into the back of the net – but once again Attwell ruled it out for a mysterious foul that not even the Forest players appealed for.

Prior to all of that the game had, for a local derby, been a little on the tame side.

Neither side had a shot on target until the early stages of the second half and Forest took the lead in the 54th minute as Tito Villa scored an unfortunate own-goal when a save rebounded off him and went in.

The Argentine levelled matters up on 65 minutes with a stooping header after Barazite had flicked on a Kris Commons free-kick but it was not until McGugan was sent off nine minutes later that Derby really started to step it up.

And then came the stoppage-time drama.

Derby: Bywater, Connolly, Leacock, Nyatanga, Stewart, Teale (Barazite HT), Green, Addison, Commons, Ellington (Kazmierczak 72), Hulse (Villa 29).

Other Subs: Carroll (GK), Zadkovich

Forest: Camp, Perch, Breckin, Morgan, Lynch, Anderson, Fletcher (Chambers HT), McGugan, McCleary (Thornhill 85), Garner (Tyson 68), Earnshaw.

Other Subs: Smith (GK), Wilson

Sent off: McGugan (Forest)

Booked: Leacock, Addison, Nyatanga (Derby); Camp, Perch, Lynch, Fletcher, Garner (Forest)

Referee: S. Attwell

Attendance: 33,010

Reaction

Not surprisingly, the verdict coming out of the Derby dressing room was that they felt robbed of what would have been a dramatic victory over their rivals.

'Bewildered' was a word used to sum up boss Paul Jewell's post-match mood and the Scouser was still shaking his head when he met with the media to give his verdict.

'We have just missed a penalty and their goalkeeper makes a great save from the corner then we score again from the second,' he raged.

'It's a great goal. You look and Forest aren't even complaining – one or two hands went up asking for something but it was a goal.

'I have never felt so aggrieved in my life, especially with the meaning of the game. It would have been a great result for everyone in a game where we hadn't played particularly well.

'There wasn't a decision to make. If it was a 50–50 call and he had given something then I can understand it, but it was 100 per cent a goal.

'It was a great ball in and a great header. This feels like a loss right now.'

Forest chief Colin Calderwood preferred instead to concentrate on the starring performance of his goalkeeper Lee Camp, who came up against Derby for the first time since leaving the club in 2007.

Camp had been named Man of the Match on Sky Sports for a string of fine saves, not just those two in the midst of the stoppage-time drama.

Calderwood acknowledged: 'A wee bit of folklore has been written with Lee Camp's penalty save.

'It was written in the stars that either Lee, Robert Earnshaw or Kris Commons would have a major impact on the game and fortunately for us it was Lee.

'We can take a lot of credit from the game, hanging on with 10 men, but I'm disappointed. I'm disappointed with the manner in which they scored. For an away team in a 'derby' we had them exactly where we wanted them.'

However, Calderwood did admit that fortune favoured his side with referee Stuart Attwell's late officiating.

He added: 'For the first time this season I think we've had a bit of good fortune with a refereeing decision. He's given a penalty that wasn't but then ruled out a goal that looked perfectly legitimate.'

What Happened Next

Derby certainly channelled their feeling of injustice in the right way as in their next match, away to Brighton & Hove Albion in the League Cup just 48 hours later, they produced a fine performance in winning 4–1 with Tito Villa netting a hat-trick to add to his goal against Forest.

It was the start of a run of three wins in four games but the back end of November saw things start to turn sour, and by the end of the year Paul Jewell had quit.

Nigel Clough, a legend as a Forest player, took over in January and slowly steadied the ship although relegation fears were not finally banished until the penultimate game of a season that saw Derby eventually finish 18th, eight points clear of the bottom three.

One place and one point behind the Rams in the table came Nottingham Forest, who had their own relegation concerns and had their own managerial change – replacing Colin Calderwood with a man whose name was etched in Derby's recent history.

Billy Davies led the Rams to promotion to the Premier League in 2007 but was relieved of his duties in November that year and had been out of the game before taking over at the City Ground just three days before Clough was appointed at Derby.

The two sides would meet three more times in the 2008–09 season with both Davies and Clough coming up against their former employers – but more of that later.

As for the referee, Stuart Attwell, having been given such a high-profile encounter at the age of 26 and following his controversial calls he was 'stood down' from the following week's fixture list.

Featured Player

It was impossible not to feel any sympathy for Miles Addison after he was cruelly robbed of what would have been a way to write himself into Derby County legend with his first senior goal.

Addison had been a fixture in the team since being called in by manager Paul Jewell the previous August, when he selected the powerhouse teenager in the middle of midfield for a League Cup tie away to Preston North End.

Though born in London and raised in Nottingham, Addison had come through Derby's youth ranks and played reserve team football as early as 2005 before signing his first professional contract in the summer of 2007.

In between those points, in April 2006, he had been called up out of the blue to make his first-team debut aged just 17 by then-manager Terry Westley, who as Academy manager had also overseen his development as a youngster.

Addison kept his place the following week but did not make another senior appearance until May 2008 and the penultimate game in the Premier League season, away to Blackburn Rovers.

What was most surprising about his call for the Preston game was that he was in midfield having only previously played at centre-half, where he had made his name at the club.

But Addison was more than at home in the Championship engine-room as he impressed with his performances and after being denied against Forest, he added his first goal two weeks later against Sheffield Wednesday, then captained the side in December while still only 19.

A foot injury ended his 2008–09 campaign early but he was back for the start of the following season, though this time at centre-back, and he soon won an England Under-21 cap – as a midfielder.

His foot problems resurfaced, to the extent that in February 2010 he was ruled out for the remainder of the campaign and all of 2010–11 as a solution was sought for an injury that at one stage threatened his career.

Addison made a far swifter recovery than expected and he was back by November 2010, adding 22 appearances across the season though most were as a substitute.

In the summer of 2011 he signed a new contract taking him up to the summer of 2013 before moving on loan to Barnsley in a deal that ran until the end of January 2012.

After his return to Pride Park, Addison was loaned to League One side Bournemouth for the remainder of the season.

Nottingham Forest 2 Derby County 3

4 February 2009

Background

It is probably an accurate point to make when saying that neither side would have really wanted this game, an FA Cup fourth-round replay squeezed in with schedules already pretty hectic.

But that is exactly what they were faced with after the initial tie ended in a 1–1 stalemate at Pride Park Stadium with Rob Hulse's first-half goal for the Rams having been cancelled out by a strike from Robert Earnshaw, against his old club.

But it is fair to say that the real intrigue surrounding this fixture came in the shape of the clubs' respective managerial situations.

Colin Calderwood had taken charge of Nottingham Forest in May 2006 and had led the club to promotion in 2008 but by Christmas, just four wins had been accrued, and a 4–2 defeat at home to Doncaster Rovers on Boxing Day proved the final straw and the Scot was gone.

Just two days later it was time for a change at Derby as the Rams lost 1–0 at home to Ipswich Town, a sixth defeat in the last nine games, so Paul Jewell handed in his resignation having spent a little over a year in the role.

All of this was unfolding before even the third round had taken place but over the coming days the favourites for the respective jobs were men whose names were etched in the history of the opposition.

Forest's job was the first to be filled and Calderwood was replaced by a fellow Scot, Billy Davies, who had been out of work since losing his job as Derby's manager in November 2007 having led the club to promotion to the Premier League at the first attempt.

By the time of his departure, however, Davies had become an unpopular figure among Derby fans and he did not help his cause after leaving with subsequent media interviews where he claimed he wished it had been Preston North End he took up via the Play-off Final at Wembley rather than the Rams.

Davies did not take charge of Forest's FA Cup third round fixture at Manchester City and instead left duties that day to caretaker John Pemberton, who was in charge for the remarkable 3–0 success away to the Premier League side.

In contrast, Derby had Chris Hutchings – Jewell's former assistant – taking the team for their FA Cup clash, away to non-League side Forest Green Rovers, and it proved a classic in every sense of the word as the Conference club led 2–0 and 3–2 on an ice-rink of a pitch before eventually going down 4–3 thanks to a late Steven Davies penalty.

Derby then moved to fill the vacant hot-seat at Pride Park Stadium with a visit along the A38 to Burton Albion and an approach for their boss Nigel Clough – the second highest goalscorer in Nottingham Forest's history and son of Brian, a legend for his unmatched achievements as manager of both clubs.

By the time of Clough's appointment, into a job that the man himself said was the only one he would have left Burton for, the draw for the fourth round had been made and pitted Derby and Forest together at Pride Park – meaning a quick return to his old home for Davies, and an early chance for Clough to come up against the club he spent the majority of his playing career at.

Davies, as it turned out, was not able to make the initial tie due to a serious family illness, but the 1–1 draw meant he would be welcoming his old employers to his new home for a replay while Clough would be returning to the City Ground.

And ahead of the second meeting, Clough admitted: 'It will be somewhat emotional and a little bit strange with it being such a big game.

'But the main thing will be what happens on the pitch and about the supporters and atmosphere they generate.

'Having played there for a few years, it will certainly be familiar. Some things have changed there over the years, a couple of stands are different now, but the atmosphere that we used to get over the years when we did play Derby will be just the same.'

Davies was also up for the occasion but insisted that his mind was purely focused on the future rather than what had gone on before.

He said: 'I've got nothing to prove to Derby County, their fans or anybody else. I'm very satisfied with what was achieved during the period I was with them – I've moved on and don't have any bitter vendetta against the fans or the club.

'It's now time for me to look to the future and not the past and it's all about keeping Forest in the Championship and then looking beyond that.'

And as if a midweek FA Cup replay between Derby County and Nottingham Forest did not have enough spice about it, there was one massive incentive to get through.

With the draw for round five having already been made the winners knew that they would face a home tie against the defending Premier League, Champions League and Club World Cup winners Manchester United.

Report

Like pretty much all local derby encounters, this game started at a fast pace but unfortunately from the Rams' perspective they were not at it right from the off.

They paid for their tardiness with just two minutes on the clock as they failed to clear a corner and the ball was played back out to Forest's Chris Cohen, whose shot may have taken a slight deflection on its way through but it beat Stephen Bywater all ends up.

Kris Commons nearly pulled one back immediately for the Rams but then Lewis McGugan and Nathan Tyson wasted good opportunities to double Forest's lead.

Double it they did, however, with just 14 minutes gone as Tyson ran clear and was hauled down by Bywater, earning the 'keeper a yellow card, and the home striker got up to fire in the penalty himself.

The City Ground was rocking with the Forest faithful anticipating a straightforward night but it was clear that this would be anything but when Derby were back in the game on 27 as Rob Hulse nodded a Gary Teale cross into the corner.

Nigel Clough's players had threatened to score before their goal and they continued to press after it, but it took them until the hour to find an equaliser.

Teale was again the architect and he cut in from the left to chip over another delightful cross but this time the head of Paul Green met it to spark off wild celebrations from the Derby fans in the Bridgford End.

From then on it was attack v attack with both sides pouring forward in search of a winner, Green going close for Derby and Bywater scrambling away an effort from the hosts' Garath McCleary.

Commons then struck a post from distance in the 74th minute but Forest failed to clear properly and the former Red made his old mates pay by carving out a chance for himself on the edge of the box and finding the back of the net via a nick off Wes Morgan.

If the celebrations for the equaliser were wild, this time they were positively euphoric with Commons the centre of attention, both from players and supporters.

The question was whether Derby could hold on and they managed to do so largely untroubled, with the image of skipper Robbie Savage waving his scarf in celebration to the fans behind the goal becoming an iconic reminder of one of the club's most remarkable FA Cup ties.

Forest: Smith, Wilson, Chambers, Morgan, Breckin, Perch (Byrne 70), McGugan, Tyson (Newbold 86), McCleary (Heath 81), Cohen, Thornhill.

Other Subs: Darlow (GK), Bencherif, Reid, Whitehurst

Derby: Bywater, Connolly, McEveley, Green, Commons, Savage, Hulse (Ellington 82), Nyatanga, Teale, Barazite, Albrechtsen.

Other Subs: Carroll (GK), Stewart, Villa, Sterjovski, Todd, Pearson

Referee: C. Foy

Booked: McGugan (Forest); Bywater, McEveley (Derby)

Attendance: 29,001

Reaction

There surely cannot be many better ways to win a game away to your local rivals than by coming from two goals down after 15 minutes and ending up on top with a 3–2 victory.

Given that the winning goal was scored by Kris Commons, whose move from Nottingham Forest to Derby County over the summer had caused plenty of controversy, the elation on everyone in black and white was there for all to see.

Commons had received merciless stick from the home faithful on his first return to the City Ground and declined to speak in the round of post-match interviews, as did Nigel Clough, despite leading Derby to their first win at the City Ground since 1971, when his late father Brian was in charge of the Rams.

Instead, coach Andy Garner was given the task of facing the media and his use of the word 'unbelievable' summed the night up perfectly.

He said: 'That was an unbelievable night. We had a terrible start, but we felt that to get the goal back before half-time would put us in with a chance.

'We said that to the lads at half-time, that it was good for them to get back in the game, we said it was there if they wanted it and the second half was unbelievable.

'We were disappointed with the start to the game but the way we played after that, the commitment we showed, we're getting there.

'The players have shown a lot of character. You're maybe thinking at two down the game is over but tonight we have seen great character in all of the players.

'When you work as hard as they have done tonight you know you have got a chance. Kris can do things like that, he's a good player, and I'm sure he will enjoy that goal for a long time.'

The feeling coming from the home dressing room was not quite so positive although Billy Davies, whose injury crisis had forced him to use several of Forest's younger players, felt there were plus points for the Reds.

He said: 'I'm disappointed at losing a 2–0 goal lead. We scored a fantastic first goal from a well-worked corner kick but once we had a two-goal lead inexperience kicked in.

'We dropped off the game, we sat off them and allowed them to put crosses into the box and when it went to 2–1 I felt that was a big turning point.

'Derby showed more experience and more know-how at the start of the second half, they moved the ball around much better and then came back into the game with a similar goal – we didn't stop the cross, we didn't pick up in the box and they had a free header.

'My words to the players were clear: be very proud of what you have achieved in the sense of who you competed against, a side that's not long out of the Premier League that has spent their parachute payment and built up a massive squad.'

What Happened Next

Defeat for Forest was the end of their FA Cup ambitions for another year but for Derby the comeback win sent them into the last 16 for the second time in three seasons – and into a home tie against Manchester United.

And the fifth-round encounter would be the third meeting between Derby and United since the start of 2009 with the two teams having already met in the semi-final of the Carling Cup.

The Rams won the first leg 1–0 at Pride Park Stadium only to lose 4–2 in the second at Old Trafford and, mindful of his side's earlier humbling, Sir Alex Ferguson sent a far stronger United squad down for the FA Cup tie.

In the end the visitors won through with a comfortable-looking 4–1 scoreline but they were made to work for every single second of the 90 minutes and had Ryan Giggs in evergreen form.

Nani and Darron Gibson had put them two up by half-time and a Cristiano Ronaldo header made it 3–0 early in the second half and, although Miles Addison pulled one back for Derby, the final goal went United's way thanks to a late Danny Welbeck finish.

So Derby were out of the competition too, although they would be back at the City Ground before February was out for another memorable occasion.

Featured Player

When a player leaves one of the great rivals the previous summer to join the other, then scores the winner for his new club on his first return to the ground he used to call home, he is worthy of a mention.

When that player is also a lifelong fan of the club he has moved from, you can only imagine how Kris Commons must have been feeling on the night of 4 February 2009.

Commons had moved to the City Ground as a fairly unheralded youngster from Stoke City in 2004 and was part of the Forest side relegated from the Championship in his first season with the club.

He kicked on as a player over the next couple of years and there was a lot of speculation about his future as the end of the 2006–07 season approached but, with Forest in the promotion shake-up, he opted for another year in Nottingham.

They failed in their bid to return to the Championship however, and 12 months down the line it was a case of déjà vu with Commons' future once again up in the air and lots of talk linking him with a Bosman move to Derby.

Commons scored one of the goals that did earn Forest promotion from League One on the final day but that proved to be his last match as, having rejected their attempts to keep him at the club, he was released at the end of his deal.

Derby moved quickly to open talks and he soon became part of manager Paul Jewell's summer revolution at Pride Park Stadium.

Having settled in at Pride Park, Commons – though born in Mansfield – received a call-up to the Scotland squad after just a few months and scored seven goals in his first season with Derby, the highlight a stunner to beat Manchester United in the first leg of the Carling Cup semi-final.

Commons was signed by Derby as a winger but reached his highest performance levels playing as a second striker, usually just off Rob Hulse, and the pair formed a good partnership.

Both had their injury problems in 2009–10 with Commons having a number of lengthy spells out of action and his impact was less than it had been during his debut campaign, but in the first half of 2010–11 he really stepped it up.

By the turn of the year he had scored 13 goals for Derby, including one in the 5–2 defeat at the City Ground, but with his contract in its final months his future was once again in doubt.

Derby attempted to keep their talisman but failed, although they did at least get the consolation of a fee when he joined Scottish giants Celtic in the January transfer window, bringing to an end two-and-a-half-years at Pride Park that could be described as 'enigmatic' – on his day the best player in the Championship, but at times hugely infuriating.

Nottingham Forest 1 Derby County 3

21 February 2009

Background

When the two clubs met in February 2009 the Rams were in a perilous position. They had played 31 Championship games and only managed to win 10 of them with a further eight points picked up as a result of draws.

No team below them had a better goal difference and no side had games in hand, but it has always been the case that points in the bag are the most essential commodity.

As a result of all this Derby found themselves sitting 16th in the table and six points above the relegation zone.

If things were not the best for Derby they were nothing compared to the problems down the road where Forest had accrued just 34 points and were down in 20th place, a mere two points above the danger area.

Inconsistency had been a big part of the Rams' season as shown by the fact that they had only posted back-to-back wins three times during the campaign.

February was proving to be both a crucial and successful month for the Pride Park side as they won three out of four games going into the final local derby match of the campaign.

The one defeat had come at the hands of Manchester United in an FA Cup tie which had seen a comprehensive 4–1 victory to the Premier League giants from Old Trafford.

Of arguably greater significance was the game at the start of the month that had been responsible for the match against Sir Alex Ferguson's men – an FA Cup victory at the City Ground over Derby's deadliest rivals.

The 3–2 win at the City Ground was the first win away to Forest since a 2–0 win in the 1971–72 season.

The Cup win had been a replay and with a 1–1 home result in the League the previous November Nigel Clough's men had the chance to go four consecutive games against the Reds in one season without tasting defeat.

Surely another victory was too much to hope for though?

Report

The midweek victory over Blackpool had left Clough with selection problems as both Miles Addison and Gary Teale had picked up injuries. Also ruled out was striker Chris Porter who was suffering with a tight hamstring.

The visitors had the best possible start when local boy Lewin Nyatanga prodded the Rams into a fourth-minute lead.

The architect of the goal had been Kris Commons who delivered a typically accurate free-kick into the box. Nyatanga got his head to it without too much success, but when the ball then fell at his feet he fired his shot past Forest 'keeper Paul Smith for the lead.

Commons, like all those returning to their former homes now wearing Derby colours, had been greeted with boos from the word go, and his setting-up of the opening goal did nothing to silence the hecklers.

Before the Rams could build up a real head of steam, injury struck and they were forced to adjust as Nacer Barazite fell awkwardly and departed the pitch with his arm in a sling and in obvious pain. Mile Sterjovski was introduced into the action as his replacement.

The Reds were already stung into action after conceding so early and nearly got back on terms in the 25th minute.

Joe Heath provided a ball for Nathan Tyson to flick into the path of Robert Earnshaw but Stephen Bywater was quickly off his line and Earnshaw fired high over the bar.

Back came the Rams and a heavy challenge on Commons by Wes Morgan provided a perfect opportunity to increase the lead. Steven Davies took the free-kick and his curling strike brought the best out of Smith in the home goal.

Six minutes later Jay McEveley went on one of his typical rampaging runs down the left. His cross found Commons perfectly but Heath was quick to get his body in the way and deny the chance.

Earnshaw was proving to be the villain of the piece in this match as once again he was provided with a great opportunity, this time by Lewis McGugan. Again the Welsh international failed to even find the target.

First half statistics suggested that as the home side, Forest had enjoyed the lion's share of the possession – however, for all that, Bywater had been largely untroubled apart from having to deal with a few balls into the box.

As is so often the case in football it is vital to make your superiority count whether it is numerically or possession-wise. Failure to capitalise when you are on top can prove fatal as Forest found out this time.

Derby doubled their lead within 60 seconds of the restart. Once more Commons was roughed out of things illegally and Robbie Savage chose to take the free-kick.

His delivery from the left found Rob Hulse in the six yard box, and the centre-forward had no difficulty in using his head to divert the ball past Smith and into the back of the net.

Commons then nearly created a third with a pass for Hulse, but Smith was able to block the shot although conceding a corner in the process.

This left Forest with some serious defending to do as Commons once again took the flag-kick and this time found Martin Albrechtsen whose header was cleared off the line.

Commons then came close to fashioning a third with Davies the lucky recipient of another pinpoint cross from a corner but the youngster was unable to find the target.

A couple of minutes later Earnshaw once more showed his profligacy in front of goal. Again with the target looming the Wales striker fired wide of the mark.

The Rams were then forced to make another substitution as Nyatanga took a bang on the nose and was replaced by Andy Todd.

With their football flowing Clough's men crafted another great move. Sterjovski and Paul Connolly launched an attack down the right. Connolly's cross from the right seemed set to provide Hulse with the simplest of heading opportunities.

But before he had chance to do so he was bundled out of the way by James Perch. It was an obvious penalty and Andre Marriner had little problem in pointing to the spot.

Davies once again showed his composure from the spot and blasted the ball into the corner of the net for his second of the year.

With the game seemingly safe Hulse was replaced by Tito Villa, while Forest were keen to withdraw both Chambers and Paul Anderson who were already on yellow cards.

Bywater was in action with 15 minutes remaining having to save a powerful Tyson drive, while Davies was close to adding to his tally with a header that beat the 'keeper but bounced away off the crossbar.

Derby ran out of luck with nine minutes remaining. McEveley pulled up in clear distress holding his shoulder. He had returned from a loan spell at Charlton with shoulder problems, and was forced to withdraw from the action leaving Derby to face the closing stages with 10 men having already used all their subs.

With a man advantage the hosts were eventually able to give their fans something to cheer about. Garath McCleary set up the opportunity for Earnshaw who finally found the target and beat Bywater.

With only four minutes remaining it proved to be too little too late, even if Perch nearly pulled a second one back in the dying seconds.

A 3–1 success was a satisfactory reward for the day's work and with so many years without a win at the City Ground Derby had tasted victory there twice in a month.

Forest: Smith, Chambers (McCleary 64), Morgan, Breckin, Perch, McGugan, Tyson, Earnshaw, Anderson (Newbold 81), Cohen, Heath.

Subs: Gamble (GK), Wilson, Thornhill

Derby: Bywater, Connolly, McEveley, Green, Commons, Savage, Hulse (Villa 67), Nyatanga (Todd 64), Davies, Barazite (Sterjovski 15), Albrechtsen.

Subs: Carroll (GK), Ellington

Referee: A. Mariner

Booked: Chambers, Perch, Anderson (Forest)

Attendance: 29,140

Reaction

Nigel Clough was clearly pleased at the way his side had begun the game and admitted: 'The way in which we started both halves was very impressive indeed – we wanted to keep the crowd quiet early and we did that, so it was a very good start for us.

'We went a little ragged up to half-time but we came out in the second half again and played some good stuff, and got the goals to kill the game.

'There is a long way to go before we are safe yet so it is absolutely vital we keep chalking them off, and the sooner we can get the points the better for everyone, we have just got to concentrate on ourselves and keep getting the wins – the important ones like today.'

What Happened Next

The victory ensured that the Rams were nine points above the drop zone. The lift given to supporters by the win was tremendous – two victories against the deadliest of rivals on their own turf in a month felt like heaven.

However, there was no similar galvanising effect on the players who travelled to Doncaster the following Friday and lost 2–1.

Apart from the spectacular run in the Carling Cup that saw the club earn a magnificent 1–0 victory over Manchester United in the home leg of the semi-finals the Rams season had not fallen into any particular shape with wins, draws and defeats sprinkled in seemingly random fashion throughout the campaign up to that point.

The pattern continued pretty much right through the rest of the season. After the Doncaster defeat they managed a three-game unbeaten run, although two of those were draws, and clean sheets seemed impossible to manage.

They achieved just three more wins after the City Ground triumph, but with four draws as well had enough to see the club safely over the finishing line.

Derby ended the season eight points above the relegation zone in 18th place, immediately above Forest who had gained just one point less.

Ironically, if Billy Davies's men had been able to pick up anything more than a single point from the two League fixtures against Derby that season it would have been Forest looking down on their neighbours.

Instead, two draws and two victories – including one in the FA Cup – gave the Rams and their supporters major bragging rights for the whole campaign.

Featured Player

Our featured player managed to court controversy wherever he went throughout his career but Robbie Savage was more a pantomime villain than someone genuinely evil.

He arrived at Pride Park with fans still easily remembering an incident from his days as a Leicester player when he went to ground far too easily for their liking and got the Foxes a late penalty.

Savage subsequently left Leicester and moved on to Birmingham City and Blackburn Rovers before arriving at Derby.

There were six years from leaving Leicester to landing at Pride Park but such was the anger he roused in supporters that they were not keen to forget.

Savage appeared though to have a bigger problem than any animosity from the fans. The Welsh midfielder was brought in by Paul Jewell during the January transfer window with Derby all but relegated.

He was already 34 and entering the final years of a more than decent career. Jewell, however, seemed to think that he was purchasing the Robbie Savage of five or more years younger, the Robbie Savage who ran all round the park, in some people's eyes like a headless chicken and getting in the face of and winding up the opposition.

As a result of being unable to do something that he had not been able to do for a little while, Savage found himself marginalised to the extent that he went out on loan to Brighton & Hove Albion and even visited Beirut with a view to signing for a club there.

Despite the public shows of bravado Savage is deep down a sensitive individual and it was clear that the more he was sidelined by Jewell the more he hurt.

Salvation for Savage came with Jewell's decision to resign after a home defeat to Ipswich Town and after two games with caretakers in charge Nigel Clough took up the managerial reigns.

Clough quickly realised that there was still a role for Savage at the club, as long as he was not still expected to be the player of five years previously.

Clough saw a player with a footballing brain and more footballing ability than often given credit for. What that 34-year-old player needed was someone to do his running for him.

Building the side round the strengths of Savage paid off and for runs of games the Rams played some very good football – although they struggled to sustain it consistently.

Savage was not without his moments of controversy. His celebrations at the end of both the City Ground matches in this month when he danced on the pitch waving a black and white Derby scarf pleased the visiting supporters and angered the home ones.

His Derby career may have seemed brief, but he played 124 games for the Rams – a total only beaten by the 172 that he played for Leicester.

Savage scored seven goals for Derby and retired at the end of the 2010–11 season to continue his media career.

Nottingham Forest 3 Derby County 2

29 August 2009

Background

Over the years wins at the City Ground against Forest have been as rare as rocking horse manure – so a match that showed a scoreline in favour of the hosts should never be cause for surprise.

The way that the game panned out, however, tells a different story to the bare statistics, and was arguably more interesting because of what happened at the end of the game than during it. Let's not get ahead of ourselves though.

The end of August is too early to draw real conclusions as to the shape of any club's season and that was certainly true of the Rams. The table showed four games played with two won and one drawn while the Reds were yet to register any victories.

Derby's only loss in the League had come away at Scunthorpe United, but they had already suffered their annual humiliation in the League Cup by going out at League Two side Rotherham after taking the lead.

If there was any pattern forming it was good at home and bad away – Forest at this stage just seemed to be bad everywhere.

Report

Despite beating Plymouth Argyle 2–1 at Pride Park Stadium the previous week manager Nigel Clough elected to make one change for the trip down the A52 with Kris Commons coming in for Lee Croft, while an injury picked up by Steven Davies opened the way for Rob Hulse to return to the starting line-up.

Even more so than a normal League match, if there is such a thing, it is important not to concede ground to the opposition in the first few minutes. Especially away from home it is vital not to concede and quieten down the home supporters in the process.

That may well have been the plan, but unfortunately it fell apart in the very first minute. Chris Gunter started an attack down the right and fired in a cross which was cleared to the edge of the box where it was picked up by Radoslaw Majewski who fired in a 25-yard thunderbolt that Stephen Bywater could do nothing about.

There were over 4,300 Derby fans in the away end, but you could hear a pin drop down there as the scoreboard showed a 1–0 advantage to the hosts with 60 seconds on the clock.

Although the early momentum was clearly with the home side Hulse had a great chance to pull the sides level, but his shot was comfortably saved by Lee Camp.

The game was flowing from end to end as first Chris Cohen had a shot from range and then the Rams took the ball down to the other end of the pitch as Stephen Pearson fed Gary Teale, but the Scottish winger fired wide of the target.

The miss proved crucial as the Reds doubled their lead eight minutes later. A free-kick was played into the box by Cohen and the flight of the ball was diverted into the net.

Dexter Blackstock, who had featured as a loan signing for the Rams earlier in his career, accepted the plaudits, but there was a strong suggestion that the ball had actually deflected into the goal off Hulse.

Derby fans thought that they had gained a lifeline back into the game shortly after as Hulse netted with a far post header. Referee Martin Atkinson ruled it out, however, having spotted a push on Forest defender Wes Morgan.

Instead of being back in the game Clough's men conceded a third before the break. This time Blackstock turned provider, pushing the ball through for Nathan Tyson to run on to and score.

The latter stages of the first half were not without chances for the visitors, but the best opportunity – a through ball from Pearson that Hulse latched on to was quickly denied by Camp who raced from his line to clear.

Action was needed at half-time to prevent a landslide. Clough elected to withdraw Commons who, in truth, had been pretty much anonymous. In his place came Croft to play on the right and Teale moved over to the left.

A combination of the substitution and whatever was said in the dressing room at half-time quickly paid dividends.

Miles Addison attempted an overhead kick that deflected off Morgan after the home defence failed to clear a free-kick. Although there was no great power in the shot Camp was wrong-footed and could only watch as the ball trickled past him and into the back of the net.

It was game on when another deflection put the Rams within touching distance of their opponents.

This time it was Jake Livermore, on loan from Tottenham Hotspur, whose shot from 18 yards ended up in the back of the Forest net after Camp had made the right decision for collecting the drive before he saw it deflect into the opposite corner to the one he was defending.

With 30 minutes left to play, the momentum had turned and it was the home team on the back foot and their supporters with hearts in mouths, while all the noise was coming from the away end.

Forest attacks were becoming more sporadic while the twin threats of Croft and Teale from the flanks was causing all sorts of danger, although no one was able to get a telling shot in from them.

Paul Green, who had scored a number of vital goals for his club, was brought on in place of Livermore for the closing stages, and Paul Dickov, who had only just arrived on loan from Leicester City, replaced defender Jake Buxton as the Rams tried to draw level.

A simmering atmosphere finally boiled over with Garath McCleary booked for the home side along with Pearson and Paul Connolly. To add insult to injury Rams coach Andy Garner was also sent to the stands.

A Pearson shot was blocked in the closing stages, and the match ended with Derby paying for their poor first half.

It had been a tremendous fightback, however, and Clough and his team ended up disappointed not to have taken at least a point for their battling second half display.

Forest: Camp, Chambers, Morgan, Tyson, Garner (McCleary 64), Cohen, Gunter, McGoldrick (Earnshaw 74), McKenna, Blackstock (Adebola 58), Majewski.

Subs: Smith (GK), Anderson, Earnshaw, Davies, Mitchell

Derby: Bywater, Connolly, Buxton (Dickov 86), Addison, Moxey, Livermore (Green 78), Savage, Pearson, Teale, Commons (Croft 46), Hulse.

Subs: Deeney (GK), McEveley, Barker, Leacock

Referee: M. Atkinson

Booked: Garner, McCleary (Forest); Moxey, Buxton, Connolly, Pearson (Derby)

Attendance: 28,143

Reaction

Despite losing the match manager Nigel Clough was understandably upbeat over a performance that had touched the bottom and hit the heights, saying: 'It's a strange feeling because we are frustrated and disappointed to have lost, but at the same time very proud of the players and how we performed.

'We were scratching our heads at half time with a three-goal deficit. Two of the goals we conceded were poor from our perspective, but we could easily have had a couple ourselves. There was certainly no ranting and raving at the break, just encouragement.

'The second half we were sharp from the off and I don't think anyone could have complained if we'd shared the points.'

For fans the magnificent attempt to overturn the 3–0 half-time score was the major positive to come from the game but was overshadowed by the possibility of punitive action by the FA.

Tom Glick, the Rams' president and CEO, said two days after the game: 'Mark Arthur (Nottingham Forest chief executive) apologised to Nigel Clough at full-time and to a number of our directors, so I believe both clubs can work together to make sure the fallout from this incident is dealt with in a professional manner.

'As Nigel Clough has already stated, he headed for the dressing room immediately on the full time whistle, as he did last season when we won there twice. So, the manager will take time to review and assess what took place.

'Indeed, there were no complaints made by Nottingham Forest about the conduct of any of our players or officials last season, so we find it puzzling that issues regarding those fixtures are being aired now in relation to the events of this weekend.'

What Happened Next

The excitement did not end with the final whistle. What happened next would go down in legend, but with a different explanation depending on whether you supported those in red or black and white.

The facts are that Nathan Tyson ran to the corner flag at the end of the game, pulled it out of the ground and started to wave it in celebration of the victory. He then ran across the pitch right in front of the visiting fans, probably with the intention of continuing his jubilations with the Forest fans in the Brian Clough Stand.

Unfortunately, whatever his intentions, Derby fans and players saw it as an act of provocation as Tyson seemed to them to be waving the flag in front of them.

Unsurprisingly, another altercation between both sets of players ensued. With the eyes of the footballing world on them it was going to be a wait to see what action was taken against the two clubs this time.

On the field, Derby then lost their next three fixtures before stopping the rot at home to Bristol City, though their difficult autumn continued and it was either feast or famine as they were either victorious or beaten, with very few draws collected.

Wins here and there kept them away from too much trouble though abject home displays against Doncaster Rovers, Blackpool and Scunthorpe United either side of Christmas set alarm bells ringing.

They did, however, pick their form up in January but were still big underdogs when Forest visited Pride Park at the end of the month with an unbeaten away record all season and no defeats anywhere since September.

Featured Player

Robert William Hulse, or Rob as he was more commonly known, was born and raised in Crewe and as a youngster was picked up by his home-town club where he worked his way up through Dario Gradi's conveyer belt of talent to the first team.

As with so many of Gradi's products he netted the club a decent fee when moving on to West Bromwich Albion after twice ending the season as top scorer for the Railwaymen.

The majority of his career was spent outside the top flight but Hulse was with Sheffield United during their one ill-fated season in the Premier League.

He was leading scorer for the Blades until a nasty leg break ended the season for him with a number of weeks to go.

Despite that he ended the term as Sheffield United's leading marksman, and it is a matter of conjecture as to whether the team would have stayed in the division with his goals to see them through to the end.

Hulse returned to the side after nine months out but failed to score a single goal in his 24 post-injury appearances.

This did not deter the Rams who were keen to add his talents to their squad with a brave forward a key component missing from their ranks at that stage.

As he had everywhere else Hulse quickly won the supporters over and later scored the 100th League goal of his career in a 3–0 win over Sheffield Wednesday in 2009.

His first full campaign for the Rams saw him voted as the supporters' Player of the Year. He even signed off for the season playing centre-half on the final day at Watford.

Clear signs that the player had recaptured his best form while at Pride Park alerted others and Championship rivals Middlesbrough came in with a bid believed to be in the region of £4 million on the final day of the summer 2009 transfer window.

Derby were keen to capitalise on his value but Hulse chose to reject the move, citing his fondness for the Rams as the reason.

It may have been better for him to have decided to go because his form after the decision was decidedly patchy and his currency in the market was never as high again.

Interest in the following January transfer window came from Wolverhampton Wanderers with an apparent offer of £3 million.

Nothing concrete materialised except for a couple of cheeky attempts to take him on loan by other Championship sides.

Hulse saw out the remainder of the season and even completed a full pre-season during the summer of 2010 then scored the first goal of the Rams' 2010–11 campaign against one of his former clubs, Leeds United.

It was to be his final goal in Derby colours as Queens Park Rangers came in with a successful though undisclosed bid for the striker.

Hulse concluded his Derby career with a total of 82 appearances and 28 goals. His final goal tally for the club was greater than at any time in his career apart from at his first club Crewe Alexandra.

He also had an excellent record against Forest for Derby with four goals in six games.

Nottingham Forest 1 Derby County 2

17 September 2011

Background

There is arguably never a good time to play a local derby. Certainly it is unusual to find both clubs riding the crest of a wave, or struggling out of a slump. Most of the time one is doing considerably better than the other.

Although it was not the case ahead of this encounter. Derby had won their first four League matches for the first time in 105 years, while Forest had only emerged victorious in one of their opening seven games.

There was also the question of stability. Nigel Clough was into his third full season in charge of Derby, with suggestions from the owners that there was every intention of renewing his contract which was due to expire at the end of the current campaign.

Forest had signed Steve McClaren to the managerial hot-seat during the summer to replace Billy Davies and despite bringing in a number of fresh faces the manager was concerned that more were required to make his team genuine contenders for honours.

There was also the spice of both managers having played for the opposition at some stage. While Clough had enjoyed the more successful playing career with the Reds than McClaren had with Derby, the current Forest boss had enjoyed a very successful spell as coach when Jim Smith had taken his team into the top-flight at first time of asking.

In one way, on this autumn day though, both teams were the same, having lost their previous two matches, and needing a good result to kick-start their season.

And in any game against your local rivals there is always an element of bragging rights and pride, with Derby looking to win the former and restore the latter having been beaten 5–2 in their previous visit to the City Ground.

That result came in December 2010 but such had been the turnaround at Pride Park that just one player – John Brayford – lined up in the post-Christmas occasion and this first meeting of 2011–12.

Report

Forest were given a dream start when during their very first serious attack Ishmael Miller and Frank Fielding tangled with each other and the Derby 'keeper was red-carded for denying what was deemed by the referee a certain goalscoring opportunity.

Miller got his shot away past Fielding but opinion was divided as to whether the 'keeper had deliberately fouled the striker or not, and the Rams' Gareth Roberts came around to clear the ball off the line.

With Adam Legzdins brought on at the expense of the unfortunate Tomasz Cwyka, who was making his first start of the season but lasted just a couple of minutes, Andy Reid ensured that the substitute 'keeper's first memories of his debut day were miserable ones by powering home his spot kick to give the hosts the lead.

If there was controversy over the Forest goal there were many in the City Ground of a Nottingham persuasion who felt that the equaliser scored on 29 minutes should not have been allowed to stand.

It started with Jeff Hendrick picking the ball up in midfield. As he skipped past Chris Cohen the Forest player went down in a heap, seemingly having slipped awkwardly on the turf.

Referee Scott Mathieson checked on Cohen as he ran past the prostrate defender and play switched from the Rams' right to the left.

Home supporters were furious that their opponents had not kicked the ball out into touch to allow the injured man to be treated, but the referee – who looked at Cohen more than once – was happy to let play continue.

The ball eventually reached Jamie Ward who skipped past two defenders before firing in a low shot that went in through a narrow gap between the near post and the goalkeeper Lee Camp.

Half-time arrived with the score at 1–1 and the home supporters expected their side to raise the game for the second half, which they did.

Reid had a couple of chances which were off target and Matt Derbyshire was within a whisker of making contact with a cross that would have led to a certain goal.

Despite Forest's territorial dominance Legzdins had a fairly quiet time in the Derby goal and was left mainly dealing with regulation crosses and back-passes.

The visitors gave notice that they were not prepared to lie down and die when young midfielder Hendrick had a gilt-edged opportunity to open his scoring account for the Rams and give his side the lead.

A cross by Ben Davies from the right sat up nicely for the Irishman to head Derby in front but somehow, though, he conspired to miss the target altogether from just a couple of yards.

Determined to make amends, he got his first goal with a fine strike from outside the box after Forest failed to clear a rare Derby corner.

Davies was again involved as he rolled the ball sideways for Hendrick to curl in a composed finish past Camp that sent the Derby fans behind that goal wild.

Supporters of the home side – and the team for that matter – could see what looked like it would be a guaranteed home win over their local rivals drift away.

By the time the winning goal had been hit Reds fans had something else to boo, the appearance from the Derby bench of former Forest striker Nathan Tyson.

Tyson had swapped clubs at the end of his contract during the summer but due to injury problems had not yet featured in a competitive fixture for his new employers.

Home fans also used the latter stages of the game as a vehicle to call for the dismissal of chief executive Mark Arthur, who one must assume was seen by the protesters as the main reason for lack of investment in new players.

Although the hosts mounted a late rally Derby were not to be denied with Legzdins finally able to show his quality with a fine save from Joel Lynch when called into action.

Forest: Camp, Gunter, Morgan, Chambers, Cohen (Lynch 32), Reid (McGugan 68), Moussi, Greening (Findley 61), Majewski, Derbyshire, Miller.

Other Subs: Smith (GK), Moloney

Derby: Fielding, Brayford, O'Brien, Shackell, Roberts, B. Davies, Bryson, Hendrick, Ward (Tyson 66), Cwyka (Legzdins 3), Robinson (Anderson 87).

Other Subs: S. Davies, Croft

Referee: S. Mathieson

Booked: Gunter, Lynch, Miller (Forest); Brayford (Derby)

Sent off: Fielding (Derby)

Attendance: 27,536

Reaction

Nigel Clough was, unsurprisingly, a very proud man on the back of his Derby side overcoming seemingly insurmountable obstacles.

He spoke to the media afterwards and said: 'In the context of the moment, and coming off the back of consecutive defeats and against the adversity of the opening two minutes, I thought it was an absolutely remarkable performance – staggering.

'It was beyond what we could have expected. I would have taken a draw at any point during the game. It is about honesty, hard work and spirit. We have got that in abundance in the dressing room.'

Steve McClaren was understandably disappointed, and even shocked at the way his Nottingham Forest side spurned the opportunity to win and win well.

'We made a fantastic start by going in front but then defended so poorly, conceded the goal and from then it was almost as though we were in shock,' he said in his post-match assessment.

'We seemed to be frightened of the situation and played with a little bit of fear, which shouldn't be the case when you are playing against 10 men.

'We didn't defend properly. We've conceded a lot of goals lately and today we've conceded two and it could have been three very easily.

'It was unacceptable and we all feel as though we've let the fantastic Forest fans down. That's the main thing – what you want to see in a derby game we never produced. We have to get back to being hard to beat because at the present moment we look like conceding goals and that's a recipe for disaster.'

McClaren, to his credit, refused to use the circumstances surrounding the Rams' equaliser to make an excuse, stating flatly: 'I wouldn't have stopped. I would have played on, it is up to the referee to do that.'

What Happened Next

The result was certainly the high point of the early part of Derby's season and it continued their impressive start, which was then backed up by two successive home games to end September.

The first saw Millwall come to Pride Park Stadium and return to London on the wrong end of a 3–0 scoreline with Craig Bryson, Jeff Hendrick and Steven Davies on target in what was a cruise for Nigel Clough's men.

Then they took on Barnsley knowing that, with the teams around them not in action for another 24 hours, a win would take Derby top of the table for the first time since 2007.

Despite an excellent performance it ended 1–1 but a disappointing October, followed by five losses from five in November, saw Derby slide right off the pace before stabilising again through December and most of January.

They went on a run of six wins from seven including the FA Cup, but just as soon as Derby's form had turned for the better it started to turn for the worse ahead of the return against Forest – scheduled for 5 February, though ultimately postponed for safety reasons following heavy snowfall.

Forest backed up their defeat with a brave performance in going out of the League Cup at the hands of Newcastle United then in the Championship they won at Watford, but abject defeats at Burnley (5–1) and at home to Birmingham City (3–1) meant it was all change at the City Ground.

Steve McClaren stepped down as manager after the Birmingham defeat, while at the same time chairman Nigel Doughty – accepting responsibility for recruiting McClaren in the first place – also stood down.

Former manager Frank Clark took over from Doughty at the top while Steve Cotterill replaced McClaren in the manager's seat and although Forest won four of the first six under the new man, their form tailed off from the middle of November.

They lost nine of the next 11 in the Championship leading in to the scheduled trip to Pride Park, though the night before the return should have taken place they were in mourning at the sudden and tragic death of Doughty, aged just 54.

The game itself was postponed anyway, because of heavy snow that weekend, and was rearranged for midway through the following month.

As an aside, in tribute to the City Ground victory, a group of Derby fans raised funds to have a plane fly a banner reading 'WE ONLY HAD 10 MEN – NEVER FORGOTTEN' over the City Ground and Pride Park on 19 November.

That afternoon Forest beat Ipswich Town 3–2 but then failed to score in front of their own fans for the next SEVEN matches!

Featured Player

While everyone was looking to ex-Forest player Nathan Tyson, making his debut for Derby, to have the starring role in this game, his appearance from the bench midway through the second half simply provided the Rams with a different attacking option and the home fans someone to boo with purpose.

Instead, one of the real stories to rise from the occasion was that of Jeff Hendrick, the Derby Academy product who had come up through the ranks to have made his debut late on in 2010–11.

A first senior start for the Rams arrived in August away at Blackpool, just days after he picked up his first Republic of Ireland Under-21 cap, and he quickly looked more than at home in the Championship, taking his chance with both hands when an injury to James Bailey and a lack of senior alternatives really opened the door.

Having missed what looked to be an easy chance when he failed to find the target with a headed opportunity from the far post Hendrick could have buckled and team resolve wilted, but instead it only seemed to spur the whole side on.

The look on Hendrick's face was priceless when he curled in what proved to be the match-winning goal with his first professional strike for the Rams.

Hendrick paid tribute to that team spirit when he spoke after the match and said: 'Jamie Ward and Theo Robinson were straight over to me to tell me to keep my head up – and that helped me a lot.

'Sometimes, people can hammer you for missing a chance like that but they kept my spirits up and made sure I kept going. The whole squad is very close at the moment and we are all working hard for each other.

'Winning against our local rivals makes it even better and it will bring us closer. The team spirit is unreal. Morale had maybe gone down a bit after the last couple of games, although we felt we played well in those matches. Those results didn't go our way but we made amends against Forest.'

The youngster, only at the start of a hopefully long career, would someday surely realise – even if he did not at that stage – how scoring the winner in a local derby game could earn him legendary status.

Derby County 1 Nottingham Forest 0

13 March 2012

Background

Had the 2012 return fixture against Nottingham Forest been played on its original date, the Rams would certainly have been favourites to take the points against their local rivals and earn a first double over them since 1972.

After all, while Nigel Clough's men had just stuttered a little bit after an excellent Christmas and New Year period, the visitors had lost their last four matches leading up to 5 February and their overall run stretched back to one win since 19 November.

That was not the form Forest were expecting under Steve Cotterill, who had been appointed as manager in the autumn as the club sifted through the wreckage of Steve McClaren's brief time in charge and looked to recover from Nigel Doughty stepping down as chairman.

In the end, none of it mattered. Heavy snowfall on the Saturday meant the Sunday game was in doubt, then on the Saturday evening it was announced that Doughty had sadly passed away suddenly at the age of just 54.

The weather finally accounted for the game on the Sunday morning and it was quickly rearranged for Tuesday 13 March, leaving plenty of time for both sides' fortunes to change – and that is exactly what happened.

Derby's defensive solidity deserted them and although they collected a 0–0 draw at Millwall in what became their first match of February, limp 1–0 defeats at home to Reading and Leicester City sandwiched a 4–0 beating away to Southampton.

Goals deserted them too with those defeats completing a run of two goals in seven games, both of which came in a 3–2 defeat away to Barnsley in January.

Encouragement came with a 2–2 draw at Birmingham City in the first game of March, when Nigel Clough's men came from two goals down, they also overturned a deficit to beat Blackpool 2–1 but failed to do so in losing by the same scoreline at home to Watford.

That left the Rams 16th in the table, while Forest – who ended January deep in relegation trouble ahead of the original scheduled date of their trip to Pride Park – found themselves two places and five points clear of the bottom three.

They were helped by a run of three wins and a draw from the five fixtures leading up to the new date, including handing promotion-chasing Birmingham a first home defeat of the campaign a week before Derby drew there.

On the Saturday before the rearrangement, while Derby were losing at home to Watford, Forest beat Millwall 3–1 at the City Ground to set themselves up in a positive mood.

'I think the low on Saturday's defeat to Watford was intensified because of the previous two results,' said Derby manager Clough in the build-up to the game.

'We had been on such a high after getting the draw at Birmingham and then beating Blackpool. So to lose two goals in the first 15 minutes against Watford was a blow. We still feel low now but we haven't got time for that.

'Come 7.45pm tonight the atmosphere will be intense. There will be 30,000 people at Pride Park and we certainly have to start better than we did on Saturday.

'There is no time to feel sorry for ourselves. We will do a certain amount of reflecting on Saturday and then get it out of the way and get ready for Forest.'

Forest boss Cotterill, leading his side against Derby for the first time, added: 'I think you've got to keep calm heads and play your game.' It's important that you don't worry too much about the stuff that goes on around the game.

'We know how important the game is for the fans and certainly won't under-estimate just how much it means for them.

'But there's a bigger picture – it's not just trying to get a result against Derby, it's also about trying to make sure we are eight points clear of the relegation zone at the end of the game.'

Report

With the clock reading 93 minutes – albeit with five minutes of stoppage-time still remaining – this game looked like petering out into a pretty routine 0–0 draw.

That was until Derby were awarded a free-kick on the left that Ben Davies swung dangerously towards the far post of Forest's goal.

Steven Davies was there for Derby, as was defender Jake Buxton, and in the end it was Buxton who got the final touch to nod it past Lee Camp and into the corner for what would prove to be the winning goal.

Up to that point, given the local derby occasion, there had not been a great deal to note down whatsoever as both sides struggled to exert any real superiority on proceedings.

The first 45 minutes could have passed without mention at all, so scarce were any clear opportunities. Derby's Nathan Tyson hit a shot wide with the Rams' only chance, while at the other end Marcus Tudgay blazed one effort wastefully over.

At least the second period did liven up a little bit. Tyson and Guy Moussi exchanged shots, though only the Forest man got his on target, then a Ben Davies cross curled towards goal and had to be clawed away by Camp.

Not long after the hour came the almost customary flashpoint as Dexter Blackstock hacked down Ben Davies, causing players from both sides to charge in with their blood boiling, but after a bit of a scramble only the Forest man was cautioned by referee Andy D'Urso.

Then the game was held up for a lengthy period as Derby skipper Shaun Barker went down awkwardly in his own penalty area while making a clearance under pressure. Forest's Tudgay and home goalkeeper Frank Fielding immediately called for medical attention while the game briefly continued and eventually Barker was carried off on a stretcher with what looked like a serious injury.

Barker was replaced by Buxton, who immediately saw a header cleared off the line from another Ben Davies delivery, before Jason Shackell volleyed straight at Camp as Derby stepped up the pressure.

The allotted 90 minutes were almost up when Tudgay collected his second yellow card and trudged off for an early bath, leading to a brief moment where thoughts drifted to the possibility of Forest doing what Derby did earlier in the season and winning with only 10 men.

They were just brief thoughts, however, and Buxton ended them before the final whistle blew – after almost 10 minutes of stoppage-time were played given the goal, celebrations and a substitution – to bring to a dramatic end an occasion that minutes earlier looked as if it would not live long in the memory.

Derby: Fielding, Green, Barker (Buxton 76), Shackell, Roberts, Tyson, Bryson, Hendrick, B. Davies, Robinson, S. Davies (Ball 90+5).

Other Subs: Legzdins (GK), Carroll, Bailey

Forest: Camp, Cunningham, Chambers, Lynch, Gunter, Reid (Wootton 90), Moussi, Guedioura (Greening 57), McCleary, Tudgay, Blackstock (Miller 76).

Other Subs: Smith (GK), McGugan

Referee: A. D'Urso

Booked: Roberts, S. Davies (Derby); Moussi, Guedioura, Blackstock, Tudgay (Forest)
Sent off: Tudgay (Forest)
Attendance: 33,010

Reaction

The feeling in Derby quarters was one of overwhelming pride at the result, particularly the circumstances of the winning goal with it coming so late in the game – and memorably so for Rams fans.

Nigel Clough felt his side warranted the three points against their rivals and speaking after the match he said: 'It was a frantic game from the first whistle, as all local derby matches are, and the crowd played a massive part tonight by creating an unbelievable atmosphere.

'With all the crosses, corners and free-kicks we had we felt it was only a matter of time before a good chance came our way, and luckily Jake took it with a few minutes left on the clock.

'Forest were hard to break down but we kept going, kept getting balls into the box and kept getting white shirts into the penalty area in search of a goal.

'No Derby team has done the double over Forest for 40 years so to do it this season is very special for everyone connected with the club.'

Clough also had words of praise for goalscorer Buxton and added: 'Jake Buxton sums up exactly what a team player is all about and we're all delighted for him personally that he's got the winner in such an important fixture.

'Jake is a very popular lad and everyone appreciates what he brings to the squad, even if he can't start every single week. He helped us keep a clean sheet and then to go and get the winner was just amazing for him.'

Buxton himself was feeling quite emotional after the final whistle and he revealed: 'It's an amazing feeling to come off the bench in a local derby and score the winning goal.

'I felt it more for my family because they have followed me throughout my career, in the rain and snow since I was 10 years of age and they have stuck with me.

'We had three or four deliveries from Ben Davies and I thought on the night his set pieces were crucial; we just needed somebody to put their head on it.

'His delivery for the goal was probably the worst ball of the lot! It was below head height, but I just managed to get my head on it and it just trickled in.'

Forest boss Steve Cotterill felt his side were worthy of a point for their performance on the night and was frustrated with the decision by referee Andy D'Urso to award the free-kick that led to Derby's winner, especially as Forest's numbers had been reduced by the dismissal of Marcus Tudgay.

He said: 'They were magnificent, the lads worked their socks off. We deserved a point, although we didn't deserve more than that. We didn't trouble the 'keeper enough.

'We were organised and we were good on set plays, but when you're a man light and they score from that area, that's what is annoying.'

The sour points from the night were the injury to Derby skipper Shaun Barker, later revealed to be a dislocated patella in his right knee and serious ligament damage, and the chants from a small minority of Derby fans about former Forest owner and chairman Nigel Doughty, who had passed away in February that left Cotterill to say that those guilty of the chants should be 'ashamed of themselves' with a formal apology issued by Derby the day after the game.

Chief executive Tom Glick said: 'We are very disappointed that a brief moment of insensitive and distasteful chanting by a minority of supporters spoiled what was a great occasion at Pride Park Stadium last night and we do not condone the actions of those individuals in any way, shape or form.'

What Happened Next

Production deadlines meant that writing work on *Derby's Days* was completed the day after the 1–0 win – though at least it gave the authors an extra chapter to include!

But on a serious note, the result left Derby 13th in the table with 49 points to their name, matching their entire tally from the 2010–11 season but still with 10 games to go.

Nigel Clough and his players then set their sights on pushing on further up the table to end 2011–12 with more progress made and with plenty of momentum behind them.

Forest were also left with 10 games remaining but had just 35 points on the board in their fight to get away from the relegation battle.

They had been in the bottom three not so long prior to visiting Pride Park but they had got themselves out of it, though their advantage over the relegation zone had been cut to four points by Doncaster Rovers' 1–1 draw at home to Reading the same night as they were beaten at Pride Park.

Their mission for the rest of 2011–12 was a simple one – to make sure they retained their place in the Championship.

Featured Player

There is not a much better moment to score your first goal in some two and a half years than the 94th minute of a game against your local rivals to earn your side a 1–0 win.

Step forward Jake Buxton to earn himself a place in Derby County folklore with the goal that clinched a first double for the Rams over Nottingham Forest in 40 years.

Buxton was a proud man after the final whistle although, typical of his character, he would have wished for his arrival on the pitch to be in different circumstances rather than as a replacement for Shaun Barker, who left on a stretcher having dislocated his kneecap in the second half.

It proved a lucky 13th appearance of the season for Buxton as he once again showed his worth to manager Nigel Clough's squad.

Buxton was originally signed from Burton Albion in the summer of 2009 having won the Brewers' Player of the Year award in the season that saw them promoted to the Football League.

Clough had taken him to Burton the previous year from Mansfield Town, his home-town club, and with Clough having moved to Derby in January 2009 he returned to the Pirelli Stadium to swoop for Buxton, knowing exactly what he would get from the player.

Buxton went from the Conference to the Championship and started Derby's first six games of the season, scoring on his fifth appearance against Plymouth Argyle, but injury problems that started at the end of August kept him out of first team action until December.

But he returned and from Boxing Day to mid-March was a fixture in the side as he formed a good partnership with Shaun Barker before sitting out the last six weeks of a debut season that saw him make 24 appearances, by his own admission more than he expected.

Injuries decimated his 2010–11 campaign, however, and he appeared just once – as an 89th-minute substitute at Sheffield United in February 2011.

Buxton's contract was extended into a third season and he was back on the pitch in November 2011 before starting at Peterborough United on 5 November, his first outing from the off since March 2010.

Used mainly as a substitute late on in matches to shore things up, Buxton's next start came at home to Watford on 10 March 2012 – three days before the Forest game and his dramatic impact from the bench.

Upon signing Buxton in 2009, Clough said: 'He will come in hoping to take his chance and give it a good go. Jake's attitude is first-class and we hope he will surprise a few people. He is one of those lads who will put his body on the line and throw himself at absolutely everything.

'Jake does not have the experience at this level but he will make up for that with the desire and heart he has.'

Those words proved nothing less than absolutely spot-on.

IN THEIR OWN WORDS

Paul Peschisolido, scorer of two goals for the Rams against Forest in March 2004:

It was phenomenal. I was fortunate that I had some derbies in my career, with Birmingham and Aston Villa, and West Brom versus Wolves, plus the Sheffield derbies. They were all brilliant and this was no different.

You could see in the build-up that it was two massive clubs, both having a good tradition of success, and it was brilliant.

You don't know how to describe it. Everyone says it was an electric atmosphere, and it certainly wasn't a let-down.

As a professional you try to not think of it (the derby occasion), you don't want to put any extra pressure on the game and approach it as a normal game, but I'd be lying if I said you didn't have it in the back of your mind.

I knew as a striker coming in to a new club that I'd made an impact by scoring on my debut, and I thought that if you really want to make an impact you beat the rivals. If you can do that by scoring a goal or two it endears you to the supporters and they'll forgive you for having two or three bad games on the basis of what you've done to the local rivals.

For me to say you treat it like any other game, you do, but deep down you know the importance it has for the fans.

The whole week at work is relying on that so they can give their mates next to them stick all week. It's definitely added spice.

You get the build-up from the press, the reporters are running their stories through the week and people are reminiscing about old matches.

I remember it being a windy day! It (the 'coffee cup goal') was just one of those freak things. I thought we dominated, we played really well, but sometimes you just need a bit of luck.

I certainly got it on the day! I remember the little coffee cup spinning, sitting upright, and the ball sat on top of it as Barry Roche went to kick it and the ball went up in the air. I just side-footed it into the open net.

I remember thinking at the time 'this is madness' and for it to happen against your local rivals is phenomenal. Then I went on to score a second, which was nice, but still to this day people go on about the 'coffee cup goal'.

It's nice to be remembered for being successful, for scoring goals, but equally to have that strange moment is brilliant.

Never have I seen anything like that in my entire life. It was just meant to be I guess – someone was smiling down on me.

When you're down at the bottom you're looking for a bit of luck, something to spur you on and get you out of the doldrums, and it was huge for that. To beat your local rivals, play well, score four goals, that gives you the confidence going in to the remaining games of the season to think 'yes, we're more than good enough to stay up'.

The following season, Tommy Smith scored the early goal (in the 3–0 win) and that was probably one of the best team goals I can remember. We built up down the right, Morten Bisgaard turned inside and played a one-two with Rasiak, Inigo has played Tommy in and he's side-footed it home.

We absolutely annihilated them that day and I think the manager was sacked not long afterwards too.

I cherished every game we played against Forest. Those are the games you remember throughout your career – the ones against your big rivals – and we won more often than not. They didn't beat us in my time at Derby, which is a pretty good record to have.

I think the fact that both clubs share success under Brian Clough gives it a bit of extra added spice having shared a manager who had success on both sides.

It's pretty fierce. It's up there with some of the top derbies without a shadow of a doubt. I had Birmingham-Villa, West Brom-Wolves, and the Sheffield derbies in my career, so there were some good ones.

I've got a lot of memories against Forest, even for Sheffield United in the Play-off semi-final when it looked as if it was going to penalties, Warnock said to get myself on there as I would be taking one.

Paddy Kenny cleared a ball up the pitch and I've done a bit of a mazy run, then had the worst celebration ever!

To be fair I've got a good record against Forest and they probably absolutely hate me!

Nigel Clough, former Forest player and Derby County manager from 2009:

I never ever scored at the Baseball Ground. I hated playing there it was such a tight ground and the crowd were so close to you that it seemed very intimidating.

I know all about intimidating atmospheres. I have played in the Merseyside and Manchester derbies while with Liverpool and Manchester City, and even tasted the rivalry in the Steel City between Sheffield United and Sheffield Wednesday.

I have to say, though, that there is no difference in the intensity of any of those games. The pride and passion that fans have for the bragging rights is the same everywhere.

The only difference is the size of the crowd. The capacity at Anfield and Old Trafford is bigger than Pride Park but don't let that make you think that East Midlands derbies are any less passionate.

There is definitely a different feeling to these games. That is why sometimes feelings spill over on to the touchline. We've seen it in recent Derby and Forest fixtures and it is because the management and coaching staff want to win it. They know the importance to the fans.

I know everybody likes to see their rivals lose, and also they get pleasure from seeing the other team struggle at the wrong end of the table, but I think at the end of the day they would rather see the other team stay in the same division than get relegated.

I think they probably think that there is more fun to be had from taking all six points off the opposition and taking the mickey than not getting a chance to play them at all.

Morten Bisgaard, Danish international midfielder who played in both games against Forest in 2004–05:

My memory of our 3–0 battering of Forest in 2004 is that we were by far the best team. I have the *From Survival to Revival* DVD and I have seen the highlights a lot on You Tube.

What I remember best are the two goals I was involved in, the first that made it 1–0 in particular. What a move.

I recall Forest having few chances other than Kris Commons shooting wide from a free-kick before half-time.

The Rams fans were amazing, and celebrating the third goal was great as I could turn around and celebrate with them after watching Rasiak scoring from my pass.

If I picked one game out from my three years in Derby it must be this one!

Alan Hinton, who joined Derby from Nottingham Forest in 1967 and became a Rams great:

The rivalry when with Forest versus Derby, or with Derby versus Forest, was always special for the players and each set of fans loved to win against the other. They were exciting days.

I spent four years at Forest, played for England two times and was the first player to play for England from Forest in 32 years. Three of my four years were good but the last one was not so good and that's why Forest sold me to Derby, plus the emergence of a wonderful young player called Ian Storey-Moore, a real talent.

Forest started their downfall to Division Two when when they traded Terry Hennessey, Henry Newton, myself and almost Ian Storey-Moore. It was most unusual to deal players to a rival club 20 miles away.

The bus journey was easy along the A52, now Brian Clough Way, which should have been Clough/Taylor Way in my opinion.

Coming home with a victory was very special. One time, Derby won 2–0 at Forest and the late John Robson scored a brilliant goal. I can still see his smile that day, he was so happy. Ian Storey-Moore missed a penalty in that game and I scored one.

I went to a dinner dance in Nottingham after the game with my dear Nottingham friend David Huskinson and we sang in the choir the Alleluya Chorus and others, and had a ball.

Clough and Taylor never put us under pressure to win against Forest. When Forest dropped into Division Two for five years the local rivalry was missed by all.

Terry Hennessey was a great player in my view and played at Derby for Forest when on the verge of being transferred to Derby. Taylor said 'no problems with Terry today, he's coming to us'.

Hennessey was the best player on the field and we lost 2–0 at home to Forest. He had no choice but to play well or the trade to Derby would have been called off.

I was lucky to live in Ruddington when I played for Forest, and Ockbrook when I played for Derby. They were great days and I have very special memories of special characters and very talented players at both clubs.

In the US, in the MLS, the special rivalries are Seattle v Vancouver and Portland. They are passionate and very competitive, with bragging rights as usual.

Roger Davies, who played in the 1979 4-1 victory and now summarises on Rams matches for BBC Radio Derby:

When I think back to that game I remember they were a very good side and were European champions at the time.

We were not playing that badly in games but confidence was a bit low because we could not seem to see games out and we had some good performances but we could not get the wins.

It was my first local derby as I had never played against them before. They had never been in the same division when I was in my first spell at Derby.

I think sometimes if you are an outsider it does not mean as much as it does to the fans and I had been used to the battles and wars against Leeds United before coming in to this one.

You would not have fancied us on the day but off we went and it went very well indeed. John Duncan scored twice, Steve Emery got one and Gerry Daly scored the other.

At the time it was another game. I was back on a loan period and it was one we had to win as we were at the bottom of the table and did go on to get relegated that season, but the win gave something back to the fans for the bad season we had.

I cannot remember much of the game itself but I remember thinking when they got their goal back with a penalty by John Robertson that it was the last thing we needed with the way our season was going but we got another one after that to make it 4–1.

Afterwards everyone was over the moon with the result and Graham Richards on the radio almost had a heart attack! The fans really loved his commentary though and it still gets played a lot today. It shows just how passionate you get during games like that.

I honestly do not think the rivalry is as deep with the players as it is with the fans and I think that is the same in all rivalries.

Players come in and out, and their loyalties are with the club they are playing for at the time, but I do not think they quite have the same passion as the fans – not from the point of view of winning, that does not drop, but I think the passion goes deeper with the fans because it goes back a long way.

I must admit that I am well and truly into it now though! I hate to lose those games and I have had some comments to me when I have been commentating there and we have been beaten. When you are winning though, the voice gets louder!

The game where we came from behind to win with only 10 men has to be one of the best wins ever over Forest, especially after they did the double over us the previous season.

These games are always very intense because the passion is there, the atmosphere is great, and they are certainly fun to work on.

Craig Ramage, scorer of the first goal in the November 1990 victory over Forest at the Baseball Ground:

I was a local lad who was Derby through and through. I had the ability as a youngster but perhaps my mental attitude was not right. I had some trouble and in the end it was best that I left the club and made a new start.

It caused me some soul searching but it worked out in the end. I had injury problems at Derby but managed to shake them off at Watford.

I was a Derby supporter but growing up Liverpool were also my team. They were the big club in those days.

My dad was a Forest season ticket holder, and there were loads of friends and family at the game. My dad was proud of me but tongue in cheek said he was gutted when I played against his team and scored one of the goals which helped Derby to victory.

I had played the previous few games but was left out of the starting line-up for this one and started as a substitute.

I was itching to get on and sample the atmosphere. I had heard about the atmosphere at such games listening on the radio when I was growing up.

I got a bit of luck when George Williams was injured early and I came on for him. I remember coming on and couldn't get straight into the game. I was blowing a bit, then Steve Chettle gave them the lead.

I remember my goal. Gary Micklewhite had the ball and I made a run for him through the central defensive partnership of Chettle and Des Walker.

I thought 'I'm going to be clever here' and I dinked the ball over Mark Crossley as he came out and he was not expecting it.

Everything was going through my head at that stage. I remember celebrating and the Forest fans spitting at me.

It may not have been the best career goal I scored but for what it meant it had to be up there with them.

Colin Bloomfield, BBC Radio Derby presenter and matchday commentator:

'Dig that one out of the net Mark Crossley. Not a chance. In the back. 2–1.'

The words of Graham Richards, a man who commentated on Derby County for BBC Radio Derby for more than 25 years. In the eyes of many Rams fans, a true icon. A broadcasting legend.

Unique, engaging, eloquent, direct, no-nonsense – he had the knack of making even the most tepid of matches sound interesting. For any young commentator, he's been a hard act to follow.

His style came to the fore whenever the Rams and Reds came together for East Midlands bragging rights. Whether that was Dean Saunders' bullet header in 1990, 'Horacio from Rosario' netting in 1998, or Trevor Hebbert 'cracking it like a bullet' in 1988, the commentary from those games is almost as legendary as the goals themselves.

In a passionate local derby, there's no room for error for the 22 players involved – and the same could be said for the commentator. Get it wrong on the big occasion, it's in the archives for good. The goal that goes down in fans folklore could also be the goal that gives the man with the microphone sleepless nights.

My first experience of working at a big East Midlands derby was on Sunday 2 November 2008. An occasion noted not for the brilliance of Commons, Hulse, Villa or any other Derby players involved. Step forward Stuart Attwell. For days, weeks, months, even years afterwards, the referee that day has never been far from fans' thoughts.

The sense of injustice, outrage and exasperation felt by 30,000 Rams fans that day was summed up by Paul Jewell. 'I have never felt so aggrieved in my life,' was the Derby manager's post-match assessment when I interviewed him afterwards.

Twenty minutes earlier, he had seen ex-Ram Lee Camp save Nacer Barazite's penalty and Miles Addison have a perfectly fine header inexplicably ruled out.

'We're sick as pigs,' he said. 'We've been robbed. It makes it even worse that it was against Forest.'

I presented the station's Sportscene programme that afternoon, alongside commentator Ross Fletcher and Gary Rowett. Just before kick-off, I remember standing close to the centre circle, facing the tunnel, as the two sets of players came on to the pitch. The roar which reverberated around the stadium was immense. There remains nothing quite like it for a sense of intrigue, anticipation and occasion.

Taking over from Ross a season later was in itself a daunting challenge. From my first day at Radio Derby, he became a valued, respected colleague and remains a good friend. His 'so, so Wembley' line from the Southampton Play-off semi-final penalty win in 2007 retains its spine-chilling, hairs-on-the-back-of-the-neck moment years on.

My first Derby win as Rams commentator arrived in January 2010. Pride Park was packed to the rafters, and celebrated as one when Kris Commons' deadly free-kick was steered in by the head of Rob Hulse. So often those two players combined to great effect, and that pairing proved once again to be the difference for Nigel Clough's side.

The less said about the miserable 5–2 mauling at the City Ground at Christmas that year, the better. Derby were awful. Nathan Tyson ran rings around an out of position Dean Leacock. Robert Earnshaw inevitably came back to punish his former club. Derby's young flair players, Alberto Beuno and Tomasz Cywka, were totally overawed by the big occasion. A sad, bad night by the banks of the Trent, that still hurts Nigel Clough and all those devoted to black and white.

Revenge arrived in the form of Jeff Hendrick at the City Ground nine months later. My best game, my best moment doing the commentary job for Radio Derby. 'We only had 10 men' was the well-worn slogan used by Derby fans for months after goalkeeper Frank Fielding was sent off inside 60 seconds. Derby a goal down, and staring down the barrel of defeat at their bitter rivals once again.

Up stepped Jamie Ward to level matters after a jinking, sizzling run which left the Forest defence in another postcode. And then, one of Derby's own, young Irish midfielder Jeff Hendrick earning legendary status to seal a stunning win.

'You little beauty' was my instant reaction in commentary. A phrase that didn't stretch the vocabulary, but summed up the raw emotion of an against-the-odds win.

It was a special day, a special occasion, and I hope the commentary did the goal, and match, justice.

Lee Camp, Derby-born goalkeeper who played for the Rams and later joined Nottingham Forest:

My first memory of local derby matches was going along to see the Rams play at home against Forest. I would have been about 10 or 11. A number of family members were season ticket holders at Derby so I went along with them.

I remember as I grew older having mates at school who supported both teams. There was plenty of banter and teasing whenever a Derby and Forest match came round.

If you asked me which if any games between the two clubs stick in my memory I'd have to say the infamous game at Pride Park that Stuart Attwell refereed, with the mayhem of the closing minutes with Miles Addison having a goal ruled out in order to allow a penalty, and then the penalty save and another goal ruled out after that.

The game at the City Ground at the start of this season (2011–12) you would have to say was memorable, but for all the wrong reasons. We had a great start with Fielding being sent off and then us converting the penalty to go 1–0 up with so little time on the clock.

Derby responded to the challenge and we could not build on what we had. It was certainly character building.

Although I was born and raised in Derby there was never a moment's doubt for me that it was a good career move for me coming to Forest.

I had left Derby to go to Queen's Park Rangers when Billy Davies arrived as manager and decided that instead of going with either me or Lee Grant as first choice 'keeper he would bring in Stephen Bywater.

It worked well for me at QPR at first but then I fell out of favour and when Forest came calling I knew it was a good move for me.

I made it as a career move. It was a big club and although it meant I could move back to the East Midlands that was never in my thinking.

The only thing that got me was the fact that some people thought I had made the move to be vindictive. I couldn't believe that, why would I risk my career to be vindictive?

A professional footballer does not have a long enough career to be like that. I knew that if I played well enough I would win the fans over, and I have played well enough to have worn the captain's armband on occasions. It's a decision I am glad I made.

I still have friends who support Derby. Every time there is a game between the two clubs the banter is texted about. You can imagine I was on the receiving end of some after the defeat at the City Ground at the start of this season!

REMEMBERING BRIAN CLOUGH

Derby County and Nottingham Forest supporters might not agree on too many things but one name is loved equally in both quarters – that of Brian Howard Clough.

So much has been said and written about Clough over the years, from his character traits to his managerial ability, and it is fair to say that his remarkable achievements at both clubs will never be repeated.

The way football has changed since Clough's day has seen to that but, even without the vast swathes of money and the completely uneven playing field created by the elite looking after themselves, surely no manager will ever be able to do what he did.

As if his feat of completely transforming the fortunes of Derby between 1967 and 1973 was not enough, after brief sojourns at Brighton & Hove Albion and Leeds United, he did the same at Nottingham Forest by leading them to unparalleled heights during an 18-year stay at the City Ground.

Forest had honoured Clough by naming the City Ground's largest stand after him following his retirement, while when Derby moved to Pride Park Stadium in the summer of 1997 a lounge at the new venue was named in his honour.

In 2002 he was an inaugural inductee into the English Football Hall of Fame following his success in the game, both as a player and a manager, and the recognition continued in May 2003 when he was awarded the Freedom of the City of Derby.

That came on an emotional day for Clough as he was taken for a last tour of the Baseball Ground – with the old stadium due to be demolished in the following months – before a dinner in his honour was held at Pride Park prior to Derby's season-ending match at home to Ipswich Town.

Clough was invited on to the pitch to be formally given the Freedom of the City and received a standing ovation from the home crowd, with the Ipswich fans also standing and applauding in recognition of a great man's great achievement.

It was no surprise, therefore, that his death on 20 September 2004 prompted a mass outpouring of grief centred around both clubs. Flowers were left at Pride Park and the City Ground along with a whole host of tributes like scarfs, shirts, banners and other messages, while books of condolence were opened to allow supporters to leave their own personal messages.

Derby's first home game after Clough's death came the following Saturday so it was deemed a perfect occasion for the club to pay tribute to their greatest manager. A special edition of the matchday programme was produced, packed full of tributes and memories, while the day of the game saw a minute's silence impeccably observed along with a parade of the League Championship trophy – won by Clough's Derby in 1972 – by players who had been a part of that side.

Forest's major matchday tribute came the following week at the City Ground when they too had former players parading the trophies won under Clough, with the players coming on to the field with *My Way* by Frank Sinatra playing – one of Clough's favourite songs.

Despite his success with Forest, Clough had remained living in Derby so it was decided that a service to celebrate his life would be held at Derby Cathedral. However, the esteem in which Clough was held soon meant that a change in plan was required – and the service was moved to Pride Park Stadium, to allow as many people as possible to be present.

More than 15,000 people attended the service and there was not a dry eye in the house as an emotional night heard heart-warming tributes from Clough's son Nigel, wife Barbara, close friend Geoffrey Boycott and former Forest player Martin O'Neill.

It was O'Neill who said: 'Brian Clough touched the lives of all of us inside this stadium to one extent or another and we'll never forget him.

'As a player I was terrified of him most of the time, but I'll tell you something – he was a man who, when you felt you couldn't run any more and that your heart was about to burst, you put in your last ounce of endeavour for.

'It's fair to say I wasn't exactly one of his favourites – in fact he seemed to pick me out as someone that took most of the rough and very little smooth – but when he gave you praise he made you feel a thousand feet tall. He was an incredible manager and an even better man.'

Also among hundreds of esteemed guests from the sporting world and beyond was Sir Bobby Robson, another of the greats of the English game, who added: 'It was an evening that I wouldn't have missed for the world. As tributes go it was great – there's no other word for it.

'Brian was a great, great manager and a lovely man. He will never be forgotten by his family, friends or anyone who ever met him.

'For one person to bring two clubs like Derby and Forest together – and boy did he do that tonight – is the ultimate tribute.'

Derby County's media department later produced a DVD entitled *Brian Clough In His Own Words* which carried interviews and footage from Clough's days at Derby, along with the memorial service, giving fans who were not there the opportunity to see the tributes paid to the man.

But the recognition did not stop there. Given Clough's affinity with both cities, there was a clamour to rename the road that linked Derby and Nottingham.

Pride Park Stadium and the City Ground are 17 miles apart with some 13 of those miles covered by the A52 – and by August 2005, that stretch of the road had been renamed Brian Clough Way with regular signs along the route in both directions, giving a permanent reminder of the man who is so indelibly linked to both cities.

Then, in 2007, it was announced that the Brian Clough Trophy would be contested by Derby County and Nottingham Forest for the first time in July 2007 in a specially arranged friendly, and every subsequent encounter – competitive or otherwise – between the two sides.

The Brian Clough Trophy was set up as another way to remember the great man's legacy and also to raise funds for charity with Derby County, Nottingham Forest and the Brian Clough Memorial Fund to nominate the beneficiaries of the profit from the game.

Clough's widow Barbara said of the announcement: 'Brian would have thoroughly approved of this trophy, to be played between two clubs he loved so much.

'It is a brilliant idea to harness the healthy rivalry of both sets of fans into an occasion that benefits local charities.'

The trophy itself is more than 100 years old but had never been used prior to being contested for the first time, at Pride Park ahead of the 2007–08 season, with more than 25,000 supporters present to see Derby skipper Matt Oakley collect the trophy from Barbara after a 2–0 win for his side.

It was a memorable occasion, marked by supporters of both clubs joining forces for a chant of 'stand up for Brian Clough', and it was certainly a night befitting the legend himself.

But it was also a huge success by raising £100,000 for charity with £20,000 shared between Derby County's 10 designated charities for 2007–08 and a further £5,000 for the Derbyshire County Football Association's charity, £25,000 for the Danielle Beccan Memorial Trust – Nottingham Forest's designated charity for the year, £25,000 to be distributed to local charities by the Brian Clough Memorial Fund at the discretion of the Clough family, and all three parties agreed to present £12,500 each to the the East Midlands Air Ambulance and NSPCC (East Midlands).

It was an emotional night played in the right spirit and with the right outcome, though all subsequent meetings between the two sides have been competitive encounters with the Brian Clough Trophy handed over to the winners after the final whistle – or, in the event of a draw, remaining with the club currently in possession.

The next meeting was in November 2008 with the two sides back in the same division and as the points were shared in a 1–1 draw, the trophy remained in Derby. However, given the controversial circumstances of the match's ending, it led to Rams captain Paul Connolly collecting the trophy from Barbara Clough after the game with his blood clearly still boiling at his side being robbed of a victory.

The overall record of Brian Clough Trophy victories stands at six for Derby and three for Forest, with two draws, including the rearranged 13 March 2012 encounter at Pride Park Stadium.

But perhaps the two most iconic and lasting tributes to Brian Clough's achievements and legacy sit in either city, one at Pride Park Stadium and the other in Nottingham's city centre.

In December 2006 it was announced that the Brian Clough Statue Fund, launched in 2005 by a group of Forest fans who were determined to see a tribute to Clough in the city centre, had raised almost £70,000 in just 18 months – smashing the original target of £60,000.

Submissions from local sculptors had been previously received and a final design of Clough saluting the fans, with his hands clasped above his head, was produced and unveiled less than two years later.

Almost 5,000 people were present at the city's Old Market Square site to see the public reveal of the statue, along with former players and members of the Clough family.

It was long felt that a lasting tribute in Derby would also be appropriate and after a campaign from a group of supporters, it was announced in April 2009 that there would be a statue at Pride Park Stadium.

However, Derby County also chose to reflect the contribution that Peter Taylor, Clough's long-time assistant manager, had made to their success and revealed that a statue of the pair together would be erected.

Clough's son Nigel, by now manager of the Rams, said of the news: 'The most important thing from our point of view, the family, was that Peter Taylor was involved in it.

'There has been a lot of individual tributes but my dad would be the first to say he would want to be sitting alongside Peter.

'Of course it is a proud moment for me but it is important Peter is in there and it is a proud moment for his family. It was a unique partnership.

'There are not too many partnerships stay together as long as they did and not too many have been as successful as they were.

'Peter was an extremely funny, warm man. It is funny because we very rarely saw them socially but at work, it was almost a telepathic relationship between dad and Peter.'

Work was carried out over the following months by Andrew Edwards, the man who had also sculpted the pitchside Steve Bloomer bust earlier in 2009 to commemorate Derby County's all-time leading goalscorer.

The Clough and Taylor families were given the opportunity to view the statue when it was revealed in August 2010, although the unveiling did not go entirely to plan as the man known as Old Big 'Ead got in the way of the curtain.

That produced howls of laughter from those watching on, leaving Nigel to admit: 'It's appropriate it couldn't get over his head.

'When the curtain came down and got stuck on Dad's head, the family all looked at each other. We said: "If it's going to get stuck in one place, then that's where it will be".'

It was an emotional moment for the families of both legends, with Clough's wife Barbara saying: 'Brian and Peter would have loved today, seeing a statute standing proudly of them at Derby County. It has been a wonderful occasion and the monument is wonderful.'

Peter Taylor's wife Lilian said: 'Both Peter and Brian would have been so proud. It is a fantastic tribute to both men, who were at their happiest in Derby. I would like to thank the fans and the club for their magnificent support and contributions.'

No man will ever have the same impact on one football club that Brian Howard Clough had on Derby County – let alone doing the same elsewhere. His legend will live on forever.

FEET IN BOTH CAMPS

Mikkel Beck

Danish international striker who joined Derby from Middlesbrough in March 1999. Beck struggled to establish himself at Pride Park and scored just three goals for the Rams before being shipped out on loan to Nottingham Forest for a month in November 1999.

Harry Bedford

Bedford started his career at Forest in 1919 and, after a modest beginning, he went on to become one of Derby's most deadly strikers. He joined Blackpool from Forest then moved to the Baseball Ground in 1925 and scored 152 goals in 218 games for his new club.

Dexter Blackstock

Joining Derby on loan from Southampton in October 2005, front man Blackstock scored three times in his first two games but they would prove to be his only goals in an eventual nine-game spell. After a successful time at Queen's Park Rangers he moved to Forest in 2009.

Lars Bohinen

Bohinen first came to prominence in English football when he joined Nottingham Forest in 1993 from BSC Young Boys having earlier played in his native Norway. Blackburn Rovers signed him from Forest two years later and the midfielder then joined Derby in 1998 but he wasn't a hit and was released in January 2001.

Oswald Bowden

Inside-forward Bowden became a Derby player in 1930 after leaving Newcastle United but he was not to have a big impact and played only 10 games over the next five years, scoring one goal, before joining Forest for a marginally more active two-year spell of 14 games.

Enos Bromage

One of three members of the same family to represent the Rams, Derby-born Bromage scored three goals in six games between 1923 and 1927 before moving to Gillingham. He signed for Nottingham Forest in 1929 but appeared just once for the Reds.

Kenny Burns

Burns had been a successful striker for most of his career with Birmingham City before being converted to a centre-half by Brian Clough and Peter Taylor at Nottingham Forest, playing a key role in their successes of the late 1970s. He first joined Derby on loan from Leeds in 1983 then returned for a year in February 1984.

Noah Burton

Forward Burton was Derby's leading scorer in 1919–20, the first season after World War One, but he only added five more to the 13 he notched in that campaign and moved to Nottingham Forest, where he had a successful career.

Barry Butlin

A locally born Derby youth product, Butlin did not really get the chance to establish himself at the Baseball Ground and after a successful loan at Notts County, he joined Luton Town in 1972. His goals for Luton prompted Forest to snap him up for £122,000 a couple of years later.

Lee Camp

Derby born and a lifelong Rams fan, goalkeeper Camp came through the Academy and made his senior debut in 2003 before making the number one shirt his own from 2004 to 2006. He later moved to Queens Park Rangers after almost 100 Derby appearances and joined Forest in 2008.

Gary Charles

Right-back Charles started his career at the City Ground and won two England caps while a Forest player. Derby moved in to sign him after the Reds' relegation from the Premier League in 1993 and he spent 18 months at the Baseball Ground, making 77 appearances before joining Aston Villa.

Trevor Christie

Striker Christie's career saw him move from Leicester City to Notts County, then to Nottingham Forest, and next to Derby, a unique set of transfers. He was an important figure in the Rams' 1986 promotion from the Third Division with 15 goals before being exchanged for Manchester City's Mark Lillis.

Brian Clough

A man who needs no introduction, his record with both clubs will never be matched. Leading Derby to promotion from the Second Division in 1969 to the First Division title in 1972 then the European Cup semi-final, he repeated the feat at Forest. Promotion came in 1977, the title a year later, and two successive European Cups were the peak of his achievements, flanked by Peter Taylor at both clubs.

Nigel Clough

A Forest legend as a player, Nigel appeared for the City Ground club under the guidance of his father Brian and went on to score well over 100 goals for them. He moved into management with non-League Burton Albion after retiring as a player and took over as Derby boss in January 2009.

Gary Crosby

A Brian Clough signing for Nottingham Forest from Grantham Town, Crosby spent seven successful seasons at the City Ground and made over 200 appearances for the club. He later linked with Nigel Clough at Burton Albion and then became part of Clough's Derby coaching staff.

Kris Commons

In June 2008, Commons became the first player in over 15 years to move directly from Forest to Derby after his City Ground contract expired. He won promotion from League One in his last season at Forest, and arguably the highlight of his two and a half years with Derby was scoring the winning goal at Forest in a dramatic FA Cup comeback.

Terry Curran

A promotion-winning winger with Forest in 1976, Curran fell out of favour at the City Ground and moved directly to Derby in 1977. Curran made 29 appearances for Derby and was on the move again to Southampton, then later in his career made another switch from one rival to the other when leaving Sheffield Wednesday for United.

Billy Davies

Davies was appointed Derby manager in the summer of 2006 and led the club to promotion to the Premier League in his first season, before losing his job in November 2007. He then took over at Nottingham Forest in January 2009, leading them to the Play-offs in 2010 and 2011 then being sacked after the second failure. Davies had his backroom team of David Kelly, Julian Darby, Pete Williams and Andy Balderston at both clubs.

Steve Devine

Full-back Devine's Derby career lasted for just 11 games in 1983 and 1984, either side of relegation to the Third Division. Most of his career was spent with Hereford United and he also played for Gresley Rovers, while he is now a physiotherapist for Nottingham Forest.

Robert Earnshaw

Derby's record signing at £3.5 million, Welsh striker Earnshaw was snapped up by Billy Davies after promotion to the Premier League in 2007. But Earnshaw scored only two goals all season and joined Nottingham Forest for £2.65 million the following summer.

Maurice Edwards

Faithful chief scout who served Brian Clough and Peter Taylor at both Derby and Nottingham Forest. He later wrote a successful book – *Brian and Peter: A Right Pair* – charting his time with the legendary duo.

Paul Evans

Former Wales international midfielder Evans scored for Forest against Derby in the 2005 draw at the City Ground, during his two-year spell as a Red. He later became the Rams' masseur under Nigel Clough and turned out for the reserves in 2010–11 before moving on to Leicester City.

Frank Forman

Forman made only eight appearances for Derby in 1894 before joining Forest, where he racked up more than 200 appearances and won nine England caps. He was in the Forest side that beat Derby in the 1898 FA Cup Final.

Fred Forman

Just like his brother Frank, Fred appeared only a handful of times for the Rams then made the move to Nottingham. He missed out on the 1898 FA Cup Final but still made more than 180 appearances at Forest and also won England caps.

Randolph Galloway

Sunderland-born striker Galloway did not have a bad record at all as a Derby player with 30 goals in 76 games from 1922 to 1924, but he lost his place in the team and a fee of £2,500 took him to Nottingham Forest for three years.

Archie Gemmill

Gemmill was an inspired signing for Derby by Brian Clough and Peter Taylor from Preston North End in 1970. He was a title-winner in 1972 and 1975, the second as captain, and a real midfield dynamo. Gemmill joined Forest in 1977 and won the league a year later, though relations soon became strained and he left in 1979. Rejoining Derby in 1982, he finished his career at the Baseball Ground at the end of the 1983–84 season.

Charlie George

George was already an icon at Arsenal when he joined League champions Derby in 1975 under Dave Mackay. He was a favourite at the Baseball Ground too, for his goals and his style, but left in 1978. He played four games for Forest in 1980, a spell notable for his winning goal in the European Super Cup against Barcelona, and briefly rejoined Derby in 1982.

George Goodchild

Not much is known of Goodchild, who made just two appearances as an outside-right for Derby in 1896 – against Wolverhampton Wanderers and Aston Villa. He joined Nottingham Forest in March 1897 then moved to Burton Swifts the following October.

Jimmy Gordon

Gordon was a faithful coaching servant to Brian Clough and Peter Taylor through their careers. He had known Clough at Middlesbrough and first joined Derby in 1969, then followed Clough to Leeds for the infamous 44 days. Gordon joined Forest in 1975 with Clough and later retired in 1981.

John Harkes

American international midfielder who joined Derby from Sheffield Wednesday in 1993. He made 85 appearances for the Rams before joining the new MLS in the States, then played three times on loan with Forest in 1999.

Terry Hennessey

A record-breaker when joining Derby from Forest in 1970, Hennessey was the Rams' first £100,000 signing. The Welsh international had played over 150 times for Forest and added style and class to Brian Clough's Derby side for the next three years.

Danny Higginbotham

The Rams plucked young defender Higginbotham from Manchester United in the summer of 2000 and he was voted Player of the Year in his second season with the club. He left for Southampton in 2003, then in 2012, in his second spell with Stoke City, he joined Forest on loan.

Alexander Higgins

Higgins is one of an exclusive group of players who appeared for the Rams in their first-ever Football League match, the 6–3 win over Bolton Wanderers on 8 September 1888. He scored 26 goals in his two years with the club before moving on to Nottingham Forest.

Tom Hinchcliffe

The inside-forward joined Derby in November 1938 from Huddersfield Town and played a handful of games after the departure of Dai Astley, but World War Two held up his career. Hinchcliffe moved to Forest in May 1946.

Alan Hinton

One of Derby's true greats, Forest's loss was the Rams' gain when he moved to the Baseball Ground in 1967. After more than 100 games the Reds felt his career was on the slide but Derby got great service from the winger, who was their leading scorer in the 1972 title triumph and helped them to more glory three years later.

Steve Hodge

Nottingham-born Hodge started his career with the Reds in 1980 and made over 120 appearances before returning for a second spell eight years later. He then moved to Leeds United, from whom he joined Derby on loan in 1994 for an 11-game spell.

Glyn Hodges

Hodges was signed by Derby boss Jim Smith in 1996 to add experience to the Rams' promotion push and he made nine appearances before being released. He was almost 35 when Forest signed him from Third Division Hull City in 1998, initially as a coach, and he went on to play in the Premier League for them the following season in an emergency.

Russell Hoult

Goalkeeper Hoult joined Derby from Leicester City, initially on loan, in the spring of 1995 and made a permanent move that summer. A promotion-winner and Premier League performer over the next four years, Hoult later went to Forest on loan from West Bromwich Albion in 2005.

Stewart Imlach

The Scottish outside-left joined Derby from Bury in May 1954 but his two years at the Baseball Ground saw the club relegated to the Third Division North for the first time. He went to Forest for £5,000 and won the FA Cup with them in 1959.

Stern John

A prolific goalscorer in the US, John moved to Forest in 1999 and had a decent record at the City Ground but financial troubles meant he was sold to Birmingham City. Later to have an unsuccessful loan with Derby from Coventry City in 2005, the Trinidad & Tobago international made a habit of scoring against the Rams in his career.

James Linacre

Goalkeeper Linacre made only two appearances for Derby before joining Forest in 1899, where he played more than 300 games and won international honours with England. His brother-in-law was Frank Forman, whose career followed an almost identical path.

Steve McClaren

An unremarkable spell as a player for Derby in the mid-1980s gave little indication about what would follow for McClaren. An inspirational coach under Jim Smith a decade later, he became assistant to Sir Alex Ferguson at Manchester United, managed Middlesbrough then led England. After a spell on the continent he took over at Forest in 2011, but lasted for just 13 games.

John McGovern

Brian Clough and Peter Taylor signed the young McGovern – who they managed at Hartlepools United – for Derby in 1968 and were rewarded with six years of service during the glory days. McGovern followed Clough to Leeds, then to Forest, where he made more than 300 appearances and captained them to the Championship followed by two successive European Cups.

Hugh McLaren

Scotsman McLaren was a £7,000 signing for Derby from Kilmarnock in 1949 and quickly became a Baseball Ground favourite, dangerous on either wing with 56 goals scored at better than one every three games over five seasons. He joined Forest in 1954 and spent 18 months there.

Stuart McMillan

McMillan played once for Derby, in December 1914, and made nine appearances for Forest 13 years later, but he is best remembered as the man who managed the Rams to their first major honour – the FA Cup in 1946, the club's first appearance at Wembley Stadium.

Dave Mackay

Perhaps the greatest bit of business by Brian Clough and Peter Taylor, the signing of the iconic Dave Mackay in 1968 helped catapult Derby to new heights. He left in 1971, the year before the first title, but was back in 1973 – after a spell in charge of Nottingham Forest – to replace Clough in the managerial hot seat and win Derby a second Championship in 1975.

Johnny Metgod

Decorated with honours during his playing career, Dutch defender Metgod spent three years at Forest from 1984 and played alongside a young Nigel Clough. He later reunited with Clough at Derby when joining the Rams' coaching staff in May 2009.

John Middleton

Goalkeeper Middleton's career began at Forest in 1974 and he was part of the first stage of their rise under Brian Clough and Peter Taylor before being replaced by Peter Shilton. That saw him move to Derby in 1977, for £25,000 plus Archie Gemmill, but three years and 80 appearances later injury forced him to retire.

Gary Mills

Still the youngest man ever to win the European Cup, Mills played for Forest in the 1979 competition while still 17 and appeared in the following year's Final too. He joined Derby on loan from Seattle Sounders in 1982 and later played for and managed Alfreton Town.

Edwin Neve

Outside-left Neve spent two years in and out of Derby's team from 1912, making a total of 49 appearances across two seasons, though his second saw the club relegated and he moved on to Nottingham Forest for a couple of years.

Henry Newton

Born in Nottingham, midfielder Newton started his career with his home club and was a great servant for the Reds. Derby came calling in 1970 but Forest would not do business, after Alan Hinton and Terry Hennessey had made the same move, and Newton signed for Everton. He eventually came to Derby in 1973 – the last signing Brian Clough and Peter Taylor made before their departure.

John O'Hare

Brian Clough had coached O'Hare in the youth team at Sunderland and the Scottish striker became his first signing at the Baseball Ground in 1967. Seven years and more than 300 games later O'Hare went to Leeds with Clough, then he made the move to Forest. O'Hare made his last appearance as a player from the bench in the 1980 European Cup Final.

Brian O'Neil

Scottish midfielder O'Neil had a short loan from Celtic with Nottingham Forest in 1997, which included a Premier League appearance against Derby. He moved to Derby in 2000 from German side VfL Wolfsburg in a swap with Stefan Schnoor but his three years at Pride Park were injury-hit.

Roy Patrick

Right-back Patrick came through Derby's junior ranks to make his debut in 1952 aged just 16, one of 50 appearances he made for the club, and he suffered two relegations before turning 20. Patrick moved to Nottingham Forest in 1959 and spent two years at the City Ground.

Henry Plackett

Henry Plackett and his brother Lawrence played for the Rams in their first-ever Football League game in 1888. Henry made 16 appearances for Derby and moved to Nottingham Forest in 1889.

Lawrence Plackett

Just like his brother Henry, Lawrence Plackett was on the Rams' team sheet right at the start of League football. He scored twice in the opening match, against Bolton Wanderers, two of eight goals he registered in 30 appearances before moving to Forest with his sibling.

Calvin Plummer

Nottingham-born forward Plummer graduated through Forest's youth ranks to make a few first-team appearances in the early 1980s. Peter Taylor wanted to take him to Derby but Plummer went to Chesterfield, then eventually joined Derby in August 1983. Six months later he was sold to Barnsley and then he went back to Forest in 1986.

Darryl Powell

One of Jim Smith's first signings after taking over at Derby in 1995, Powell gave Derby seven years of excellent service as a promotion-winner and Premier League regular.

Powell is the last man to make 200 Derby appearances and was released in 2002 after relegation. His playing career ended in 2005 after a 13-game spell with Forest, including an outing against the Rams.

Alf Quantrill

Quantrill's Derby career was interrupted by World War One after he made his debut in 1914, but he was good enough to come back after hostilities and play in the First Division then win England caps. The son-in-law of Rams legend Steve Bloomer, Quantrill spent two more seasons in the Derby team and after spells at other clubs, joined Forest in 1930.

John Robertson

Robertson was one of the architects of Forest's successes in the late 1970s and early 1980s, scoring the winning goal in the 1980 European Cup Final. His disputed move to Derby in 1983 contributed to the breakdown in relations between Brian Clough and Peter Taylor. After two unsuccessful years at Derby, including relegation, Robertson returned to Forest in 1985.

Dean Saunders

Derby's first £1 million player, Saunders was a prolific goalscorer at the Baseball Ground and of his 57 goals for the Rams, one was a memorable headed winner against Forest in 1990. Saunders continued to score goals throughout his career – including one against Derby when he joined Forest in 1996.

John Sheridan

A defender with Notts County for most of his career, Sheridan finished playing with Hartlepools United under Brian Clough and Peter Taylor, who then took him to the Baseball Ground as a coach. Sheridan also moved to the City Ground when the duo joined Forest later in the 1970s.

Peter Shilton

One of the greatest goalkeepers to have ever graced the game, Shilton won the Football League, two European Cups and countless other domestic honours during his five years with Nottingham Forest. He joined Derby upon the Rams' promotion to the First Division in 1987 and added more than 200 appearances on his way to a grand career total of 1,237 matches – plus a record 125 for England.

Steve Sutton

Born in the Derbyshire village of Hartington, Sutton started out at Nottingham Forest as understudy to Peter Shilton but eventually won a place and made over 250 appearances, while also having a loan with Derby in 1985. He then joined Derby in 1992 and was in and out of the team, competing first with Martin Taylor and then Russell Hoult, before being released in 1996. He is now Forest's goalkeeping coach.

Peter Taylor

One half of the greatest managerial duo of all time, Taylor was Brian Clough's trusted assistant at Derby and Nottingham Forest. He was alongside Clough for all of the big successes and retired in 1982, though later that year he returned to football as manager at Derby. Although Taylor's two years in charge at the Baseball Ground were not a success for the club, he did oversee the famous 1983 FA Cup giant-killing against the Reds.

Colin Todd

A record signing for Derby at £175,000 – also a British record for a defender – when joining from Sunderland in 1971, Todd is one of Derby's true greats. He was a fixture in the title-winning season of 1972, and was PFA Players' Player of the Year when Derby repeated the feat three years later. Todd played for Forest from 1982 to 1984, and returned to Derby as assistant manager in 2000 then took over for a short, unsuccessful period as boss before being replaced by John Gregory.

Marcus Tudgay

Tudgay came through the Derby Academy and made his professional debut in 2002, going on to make almost 100 first-team appearances – including scoring against Forest in a 4–2 victory in March 2004. He joined Forest in November 2010 from Sheffield Wednesday, then notched two in a City Ground victory over Derby a month later.

Nathan Tyson

Tyson made the rare – certainly in modern times – move from Nottingham to Derby in the summer of 2011 when joining the Rams at the end of his Reds contract, after over 200 appearances for the City Ground club. Injuries held up his Derby debut until the Rams' visit to Forest in September 2011, when he made his bow as a substitute.

Darren Wassall

Starting out his career with Forest, Wassall made the direct switch to Derby in 1992 for £600,000. An underrated centre-half during his time at the Baseball Ground, Wassall made over 100 appearances and helped the Rams to promotion in 1996. He returned to Derby in 2009 to head up the club's Academy.

Frank Wignall

Powerful striker Wignall had won England caps and scored goals at a healthy rate during his time with Nottingham Forest in the 1960s, though he joined Derby from Everton in 1969 and helped Brian Clough's side to promotion that season. Wignall contributed to the 1972 title campaign despite joining Mansfield Town in November 1971.

Harold Wightman

Wightman had played almost 200 games for Derby, either as a centre-half or full-back, having joined in May 1919 after playing wartime football for Forest. He was appointed manager at the City Ground in 1936, the first man to hold that position for the club.

Alan Wright

Only with both Derby and Forest on temporary loan spells from Sheffield United, the Rams in 2006 and the Reds a year later, Wright showed all his years of experience for both clubs. Wright played his last career game for Fleetwood Town in April 2011, and in February 2012 was named assistant to fellow former Ram Paul Simpson at non-League Northwich Victoria.

STATISTICALLY SPEAKING

The Full List of Games

1 October 1892 – Division One
Derby County 2 Nottingham Forest 3
Scorers: A. Goodall, Bloomer
Line-up: Robinson, Methven, Staley, Cox, A. Goodall, Roulstone, Ekins, McLachlan, J. Goodall, McMillan, Bloomer.
Attendance: 8,500

28 January 1893 – Division One
Nottingham Forest 1 Derby County 0
Line-up: Robinson, Methven, Leiper, Hickinbottom, A. Goodall, Roulstone, Mills, Bloomer, J. Goodall, McMillan, Little.
Attendance: 12,000

9 December 1893 – Division One
Derby County 3 Nottingham Forest 4
Scorers: A. Goodall, Bloomer, McMillan
Line-up: Dockery, Methven, Staley, Hickinbottom, A. Goodall, Docherty, Allan, Bloomer, J. Goodall, McMillan, Towie.
Attendance: 6,500

30 December 1893 – Division One
Nottingham Forest 4 Derby County 2
Scorers: Bloomer, J. Goodall
Line-up: Robinson, Methven, Leiper, Cox, A. Goodall, Hickinbottom, Allan, Bloomer, J. Goodall, McMillan, Keay.
Attendance: 8,000

8 September 1894 – Division One
Derby County 4 Nottingham Forest 2
Scorers: McMillan (2), Bloomer, Raybould
Line-up: Robinson, Methven, Leiper, Cox, A. Goodall, Forman, Raybould, Allan, J. Goodall, McMillan, Bloomer.
Attendance: 6,000

3 November 1894 – Division One
Nottingham Forest 2 Derby County 1
Scorer: A. Goodall
Line-up: Robinson, Methven, Leiper, Cox, Forman, Docherty, Raybould, A. Goodall, J. Goodall, McMillan, Bloomer.
Attendance: 8,000

5 October 1895 – Division One
Nottingham Forest 2 Derby County 5
Scorers: Bloomer (3), McQueen, Stevenson
Line-up: Robinson, Methven, Staley, Cox, A. Goodall, Kinsey, J. Goodall, Bloomer, Miller, Stevenson, McQueen.
Attendance: 12,000

7 December 1895 – Division One
Derby County 4 Nottingham Forest 0
Scorers: Bloomer (3), Miller
Line-up: Robinson, Methven, Leiper, Cox, A. Goodall, Kinsey, J. Goodall, Bloomer, Miller, Stevenson, McQueen.
Attendance: 6,000

5 September 1896 – Division One
Derby County 1 Nottingham Forest 1
Scorer: Stevenson
Line-up: Robinson, Methven, Leiper, Cox, A. Goodall, Kinsey, J. Goodall, Bloomer, Miller, Stevenson, McQueen.
Attendance: 5,500

18 November 1896 – Division One
Nottingham Forest 1 Derby County 2
Scorers: Bloomer, Stevenson
Line-up: Robinson, Methven, Leiper, Cox, A. Goodall, Turner, J. Goodall, Bloomer, Miller, Stevenson, McQueen.
Attendance: 5,000

30 October 1897 – Division One
Nottingham Forest 3 Derby County 4
Scorers: Maconnachie (2), A. Goodall, Bloomer
Line-up: Fryer, Methven, Leiper, Cox, A. Goodall, Turner, Maconnachie, Bloomer, J. Goodall, Stevenson, McQueen.
Attendance: 10,000

11 April 1898 – Division One
Derby County 5 Nottingham Forest 0
Scorers: Bloomer (3), Boag, Turner
Line-up: Fryer, Methven, Leiper, Cox, A. Goodall, Turner, J. Goodall, Bloomer, Boag, Stevenson, McQueen.
Attendance: 12,000

16 April 1898 – FA Cup Final (played at Crystal Palace)

Nottingham Forest 3 Derby County 1
Scorer: Bloomer
Line-up: Fryer, Methven, Leiper, Cox, A. Goodall, Turner, J. Goodall, Bloomer, Boag, Stevenson, McQueen.
Attendance: 62,017

17 December 1898 – Division One

Nottingham Forest 3 Derby County 3
Scorers: Cox, Bloomer, Rutherford
Line-up: Fryer, Methven, Staley, Cox, A. Goodall, May, Bosworth, Richards, Bloomer, Rutherford, Allen.
Attendance: 8,000

20 April 1899 – Division One

Derby County 2 Nottingham Forest 0
Scorers: Bloomer (2)
Line-up: Fryer, Kifford, Staley, Cox, Paterson, Leckie, Arkesden, Bloomer, Boag, MacDonald, Cooke.
Attendance: 3,000

28 October 1899 – Division One

Derby County 2 Nottingham Forest 2
Scorers: Bloomer, Wombwell
Line-up: Fryer, Methven, Leiper, Leckie, A. Goodall, May, Wombwell, Bloomer, Boag, Arkesden, Cooke.
Attendance: 12,000

3 March 1900 – Division One

Nottingham Forest 4 Derby County 1
Scorer: Bloomer
Line-up: Fryer, Methven, Staley, Leckie, A. Goodall, May, Wombwell, Bloomer, Boag, Arkesden, McQueen.
Attendance: 10,000

10 November 1900 – Division One

Nottingham Forest 1 Derby County 0
Line-up: Fryer, Methven, Blackett, May, A. Goodall, Leckie, Crawford, Wombwell, Boag, Shanks, McQueen.
Attendance: 17,000

16 March 1901 – Division One

Derby County 0 Nottingham Forest 0
Line-up: Fryer, Methven, Morris, Warren, A. Goodall, Leckie, Crawford, Bloomer, O'Rourke, Wombwell, Haslam.
Attendance: 12,000

2 November 1901 – Division One
Derby County 1 Nottingham Forest 1
Scorer: Bloomer
Line-up: Fryer, Methven, Morris, May, A. Goodall, Leckie, Crawford, Bloomer, Balkwill, Warren, Wombwell.
Attendance: 13,000

1 March 1902 – Division One
Nottingham Forest 3 Derby County 1
Scorer: Bloomer
Line-up: Fryer, Methven, Morris, Haslam, Lloyd, Leckie, Wombwell, Bloomer, Boag, May, Davis.
Attendance: 8,000

20 September 1902 – Division One
Nottingham Forest 2 Derby County 3
Scorers: Bloomer (2), York
Line-up: Fryer, Methven, Morris, May, A. Goodall, Leckie, Turner, Bloomer, York, Warren, Middleton.
Attendance: 20,000

17 January 1903 – Division One
Derby County 0 Nottingham Forest 1
Line-up: Fryer, Methven, Morris, Leckie, A. Goodall, Warren, Turner, Bloomer, Warrington, Richards, G. Davis.
Attendance: 10,000

14 November 1903 – Division One
Derby County 2 Nottingham Forest 6
Scorers: Hall, Bloomer
Line-up: Whittaker, Hickling, Morris, Warren, Hall, May, Mercer, Bloomer, Hodgkinson, Richards, G. Davis.
Attendance: 7,000

12 March 1904 – Division One
Nottingham Forest 5 Derby County 1
Scorer: Barker
Line-up: Maskrey, Methven, Morris, Warren, Hall, May, Parnell, Barker, Warrington, Richards, Middleton.
Attendance: 10,000

29 October 1904 – Division One
Nottingham Forest 0 Derby County 1
Scorer: Barker
Line-up: Maskrey, Methven, Morris, Warren, McAllister, Richards, Hounsfield, Bloomer, Hunt, Barker, Middleton.
Attendance: 15,000

25 February 1905 – Division One
Derby County 3 Nottingham Forest 2
Scorers: G. Davis, Hall, Fletcher
Line-up: Maskrey, Methven, Morris, Warren, Hall, Saunders, Hounsfield, Fletcher, Hunt, Richards, G. Davis.
Attendance: 5,000

26 December 1905 – Division One
Derby County 2 Nottingham Forest 2
Scorers: Fletcher, Wheatcroft
Line-up: Maskrey, Methven, Morris, Warren, Hall, A. Wood, J. Davis, Wheatcroft, Fletcher, Paton, Middleton.
Attendance: 15,000

17 April 1906 – Division One
Nottingham Forest 0 Derby County 0
Line-up: Smith, Warren, Nicholas, Richards, Hall, A. Wood, J. Davis, J. Wood, Wheatcroft, Hardcastle, Lamb.
Attendance: 12,000

13 March 1909 – FA Cup Fourth Round
Derby County 3 Nottingham Forest 0
Scorers: Bentley (3)
Line-up: Scattergood, Nicholas, Morris, Barbour, Bagshaw, Richards, Thompson, Garry, Bentley, Barnes, J. Davis.
Attendance: 16,000

26 December 1911 – Division Two
Nottingham Forest 1 Derby County 3
Scorers: Bloomer, Bauchop, Leonard
Line-up: Scattergood, Atkin, Betts, Bagshaw, Buckley, Richards, Grimes, Bloomer, Leonard, Bauchop, Sharpe.
Attendance: 33,500

9 April 1912 – Division Two
Derby County 1 Nottingham Forest 0
Scorer: Leonard
Line-up: Scattergood, Atkin, Betts, Barbour, Buckley, Garry, Grimes, Bloomer, Leonard, Barnes, Sharpe.
Attendance: 14,000

25 December 1914 – Division Two
Nottingham Forest 2 Derby County 2
Scorers: Leonard, Moore
Line-up: Lawrence, Atkin, Barbour, Walker, Eadie, Bagshaw, Grimes, Benfield, Leonard, Moore, Baker.
Attendance: 15,000

26 December 1914 – Division Two
Derby County 1 Nottingham Forest 0
Scorer: Leonard
Line-up: Lawrence, Atkin, Barbour, Walker, Bagshaw, Brooks, Grimes, Benfield, Leonard, Moore, Quantrill.
Attendance: 14,000

24 September 1921 – Division Two
Derby County 1 Nottingham Forest 2
Scorer: Paterson
Line-up: Lawrence, Chandler, Ritchie, McLaverty, Rance, Storer, Thornewell, Abdallah, Paterson, Moore, Barnes.
Attendance: 22,803

1 October 1921 – Division Two
Nottingham Forest 3 Derby County 0
Line-up: Lawrence, Chandler, Ritchie, McLaverty, Wightman, Storer, Thornewell, Keetley, Paterson, Moore, Pattison.
Attendance: 28,000

26 September 1925 – Division Two
Nottingham Forest 1 Derby County 2
Scorers: Thoms, Murphy
Line-up: Olney, Wightman, Crilly, McIntyre, Thoms, Plackett, Thornewell, Whitehouse, Bedford, Storer, Murphy.
Attendance: 19,549

6 February 1926 – Division Two
Derby County 2 Nottingham Forest 0
Scorers: Hart, Murphy
Line-up: Olney, Wightman, Ritchie, McIntyre, Thoms, Plackett, Smith, Keetley, Hart, Storer, Murphy.
Attendance: 19,076

28 January 1928 – FA Cup Fourth Round
Derby County 0 Nottingham Forest 0
Line-up: Wilkes, Carr, Robson, Scott, O'Brien, Storer, Crooks, Whitehouse, Bedford, Stephenson, Mee.
Attendance: 22,594

1 February 1928 – FA Cup Fourth-Round Replay
Nottingham Forest 2 Derby County 0
Line-up: Wilkes, Carr, Robson, Scott, O'Brien, Storer, Crooks, Whitehouse, Bedford, Stephenson, Mee.
Attendance: 35,625

25 January 1936 – FA Cup Fourth Round
Derby County 2 Nottingham Forest 0
Scorers: Halford, Bowers
Line-up: Kirby, Udall, Jessop, Nicholas, Barker, Keen, Crooks, Napier, Bowers, Ramage, Halford.
Attendance: 37,830

7 November 1953 – Division Two
Nottingham Forest 4 Derby County 2
Scorers: McLaren, Wilkins
Line-up: Middleton, Mozley, Savin, Walker, Oliver, Mays, Parry, McLaren, Wilkins, Dunn, Law.
Attendance: 31,397

10 April 1954 – Division Two
Derby County 1 Nottingham Forest 2
Scorer: Powell
Line-up: Webster, Barrowcliffe, Savin, Bell, Oliver, Musson, R. Harrison, T. Powell, Parry, Dunn, Law.
Attendance: 21,961

13 November 1954 – Division Two
Nottingham Forest 3 Derby County 0
Line-up: Webster, Mozley, Savin, Bell, Young, Upton, McQuillan, Dunn, Pye, T. Powell, Imlach.
Attendance: 16,652

2 April 1955 – Division Two
Derby County 1 Nottingham Forest 2
Scorer: Young
Line-up: Webster, Patrick, Barrowcliffe, T. Powell, Young, Upton, K. Harrison, Parry, Buchanan, Ackerman, Imlach.
Attendance: 18,722

29 November 1969 – Division One
Derby County 0 Nottingham Forest 2
Line-up: Green, Webster, Robson, Durban, McFarland, Mackay, McGovern, Carlin, O'Hare, Hector, Hinton.
Attendance: 38,225

14 March 1970 – Division One
Nottingham Forest 1 Derby County 3
Scorers: Durban, O'Hare, O'Kane (own-goal)
Line-up: Green, Webster, Robson, Hennessey, McFarland, Mackay, Durban, Carlin, O'Hare, Wignall, Hinton.
Attendance: 42,074

28 November 1970 – Division One
Nottingham Forest 2 Derby County 4
Scorers: McGovern, O'Hare, Wignall, Gemmill
Line-up: Green, Webster, Robson, Durban, Hennessey, Mackay, McGovern, Wignall, O'Hare, Hector, Gemmill.
Attendance: 30,359

13 March 1971 – Division One
Derby County 1 Nottingham Forest 2
Scorer: Hector
Line-up: Boulton, Webster, Richardson, Todd, McFarland, Mackay, Gemmill, Wignall, O'Hare, Hector, Hinton.
Attendance: 34,857

30 October 1971 – Division One
Nottingham Forest 0 Derby County 2
Scorers: Robson, Hinton
Line-up: Boulton, Webster, Robson, S. Powell, McFarland, Todd, McGovern, Gemmill, O'Hare, Hector, Hinton.
Attendance: 37,170

19 February 1972 – Division One
Derby County 4 Nottingham Forest 0
Scorers: Hinton (2), Hector, O'Hare
Line-up: Boulton, Webster, Robson, Durban, McFarland, Todd, McGovern, Gemmill, O'Hare, Hector, Hinton.
Attendance: 31,801

27 August 1977 – Division One
Nottingham Forest 3 Derby County 0
Line-up: Boulton, Langan, Nish, Daly, McFarland (Webster), Todd, S. Powell, Gemmill, Hales, Hector, Hughes.
Attendance: 28,807

14 January 1978 – Division One
Derby County 0 Nottingham Forest 0
Line-up: Middleton, Langan, Buckley, Rioch, Daniel, Todd, Curran, Daly, Masson, George, Ryan (S. Powell).
Attendance: 33,384

26 December 1978 – Division One
Nottingham Forest 1 Derby County 1
Scorer: Daly
Line-up: McKellar, Langan, Buckley, Daly, McFarland, Webb, Carter (Moreland), S. Powell, Caskey, Clark, Hill.
Attendance: 34,256

14 April 1979 - Division One
Derby County 1 Nottingham Forest 2
Scorer: Webb
Line-up: McKellar, Langan, Buckley, Moreland, Webb, Wicks, Carter, S. Powell, Greenwood, Emson, Crawford.
Attendance: 30,156

24 November 1979 - Division One
Derby County 4 Nottingham Forest 1
Scorers: Duncan (2), Emery, Daly
Line-up: McKellar. Langan, Buckley, Daly (Emson), Webb, Osgood, Emery, B. Powell, Duncan, Davies, Clark.
Attendance: 27,729

19 April 1980 - Division One
Nottingham Forest 1 Derby County 0
Line-up: McKellar, Langan, Buckley, McCaffery, McFarland, Osgood, S. Powell, B. Powell, Biley, Swindlehurst, Wilson (Emson).
Attendance: 32,266

8 January 1983 - FA Cup Third Round
Derby County 2 Nottingham Forest 0
Scorers: Gemmill, Hill
Line-up: Cherry, Barton, Attley, Gemmill (Dalziel), Foster, McAlle, Brolly, Wilson, Hill, Swindlehurst, Mills.
Attendance: 28,494

30 October 1985 - League Cup Third Round
Derby County 1 Nottingham Forest 2
Scorer: Chandler
Line-up: Wallington, Palmer, Buckley, Williams (Garner), Hindmarch, MacLaren, Micklewhite, Christie, Davison, McClaren, Chandler.
Attendance: 22,226

October 10 1987 - Division One
Derby County 0 Nottingham Forest 1
Line-up: Shilton, Sage (MacLaren), Forsyth, Williams, Wright, Blades, Callaghan, Gee, Garner, Gregory, Cross.
Attendance: 22,394

30 March 1988 - Division One
Nottingham Forest 2 Derby County 1
Scorer: Foster (own-goal)
Line-up: Shilton, Blades, Forsyth, Williams, Wright, Hindmarch (MacLaren), Stapleton, Lewis (Micklewhite), Gee, Gregory, Callaghan.
Attendance: 25,017

17 September 1988 – Division One
Nottingham Forest 1 Derby County 1
Scorer: Hebberd
Line-up: Shilton, Sage, Forsyth, Williams, Wright, Blades, McMinn, Gee (Cross), Goddard, Hebberd, Callaghan.
Attendance: 24,818

25 March 1989 – Division One
Derby County 0 Nottingham Forest 2
Line-up: Shilton, Blades, Forsyth, Williams, Wright, Hindmarch, McMinn, Saunders, Gee (Cross), Hebberd, Micklewhite.
Attendance: 25,174

30 August 1989 – Division One
Nottingham Forest 2 Derby County 1
Scorer: Hodge (own-goal)
Line-up: Shilton, Blades, Forsyth, Williams, Wright, Hindmarch, McMinn (Cross), Saunders, Goddard (Gee), Hebberd, Micklewhite.
Attendance: 24,060

20 January 1990 – Division One
Derby County 0 Nottingham Forest 2
Line-up: Shilton, Sage, Forsyth, Williams, Wright, Hindmarch, Pickering (Francis), Saunders, Harford, Hebberd, Patterson (McCord).
Attendance: 24,190

24 November 1990 – Division One
Derby County 2 Nottingham Forest 1
Scorers: Ramage, Saunders
Line-up: Shilton, Patterson, Pickering, G. Williams (Ramage), Wright, Forsyth, Micklewhite, Saunders, Harford, Hebberd, Callaghan.
Attendance: 21,729

10 April 1991 – Division One
Nottingham Forest 1 Derby County 0
Line-up: Shilton, Sage, Cross, G. Williams, Wright (Kavanagh), Forsyth, Micklewhite, Saunders, Harford, Wilson, McMinn (P. Williams).
Attendance: 25,109

18 August 1993 – First Division
Nottingham Forest 1 Derby County 1
Scorer: Forsyth
Line-up: Taylor, Charles, Forsyth, Kuhl, Short, Wassall, Harkes, Williams, Kitson, Gabbiadini, Pembridge.
Attendance: 26,684

8 September 1993 – Anglo-Italian Cup Preliminary Round
Derby County 3 Nottingham Forest 2
Scorers: Simpson, Kitson, Kuhl
Line-up: Taylor, Charles, Forsyth, Kuhl, Short, Wassall, Johnson, Williams, Kitson, Gabbiadini, Simpson.
Subs: Sutton, Chalk, Kavanagh.
Attendance: 6,654

27 April 1994 – First Division
Derby County 0 Nottingham Forest 2
Line-up: Taylor, Charles (Kavanagh), Nicholson (Hayward), Harkes, Short, Williams, Cowans, Gabbiadini, Kitson, Pembridge, Simpson.
Attendance: 19,300

19 October 1996 – Premier League
Nottingham Forest 1 Derby County 1
Scorer: Dailly
Line-up: Hoult, C. Powell, Rowett, Dailly, Stimac, Laursen (Carsley), Asanovic, D. Powell, Ward (Carbon), Willems (Simpson), McGrath.
Other subs: Quy, Flynn.
Attendance: 27,771

23 April 1997 – Premier League
Derby County 0 Nottingham Forest 0
Line-up: Taylor, Rowett, C. Powell, van der Laan, Sturridge, Asanovic, Trollope, Laursen, Carsley, Dally, Wanchope (Ward).
Other subs: Willems, Simpson, Solis, Hoult.
Attendance: 18,087

16 November 1998 – Premier League
Nottingham Forest 2 Derby County 2
Scorers: Dorigo (pen), Carbonari
Line-up: Hoult (Poom), Carbonari, D. Powell, Dorigo, Wanchope, Harper (Sturridge), Laursen, Bohinen, Prior, Elliott, Burton.
Other subs: Baiano, Eranio, Bridge-Wilkinson.
Attendance: 24,014

10 April 1999 – Premier League
Derby County 1 Nottingham Forest 0
Scorer: Carbonari
Line-up: Hoult (sent off), Prior, Carbonari, Laursen, Borbokis (Sturridge), D. Powell, Bohinen, Baiano (Harper), Schnoor, Wanchope, Burton (Poom).
Other subs: Dorigo, Elliott.
Attendance: 32,217

20 October 2002 – Division One
Derby County 0 Nottingham Forest 0
Line-up: Grant, Hunt, Riggott, Evatt, Higginbotham, Boertien, Murray (Kinkladze), Lee, Bolder, Christie, McLeod.
Other subs: Elliott, Morris, Oakes, Twigg.
Attendance: 30,547

19 March 2003 – Division One
Nottingham Forest 3 Derby County 0
Line-up: Grant, Barton, Mills, Elliott, Boertien (Zavagno), Burley, Lee, Bolder, McLeod, Mooney, Ravanelli (Chadwick).
Other subs: Hunt, Kinkladze, Oakes.
Attendance: 29,725

27 September 2003 – Division One
Nottingham Forest 1 Derby County 1
Scorer: Junior
Line-up: Oakes, Jackson, Mills, Johnson, Zavagno, Valakari (Caldwell), Huddlestone, Taylor, Holmes (Costa), Junior (Morris), Svensson.
Other subs: Boertien, Grant.
Attendance: 29,059

20 March 2004 – Division One
Derby County 4 Nottingham Forest 2
Scorers: Taylor, Peschisolido (2), Tudgay
Line-up: Grant, Kenna, Mawene, Johnson, Jackson (Boertien), Costa (Holmes), Taylor, Huddlestone, Osman, Tudgay, Peschisolido.
Other subs: Whelan, Oakes, Labarthe Tome.
Attendance: 32,390

11 December 2004 – Championship
Derby County 3 Nottingham Forest 0
Scorers: Smith, Rasiak (2)
Line-up: Camp, Kenna, Huddlestone, Johnson (Bolder), Jackson, Smith, Taylor, Idiakez, Bisgaard, Rasiak (Mills), Peschisolido (Reich).
Other subs: Grant, Tudgay.
Attendance: 30,793

26 February 2005 – Championship
Nottingham Forest 2 Derby County 2
Scorer: Rasiak (2)
Line-up: Camp, Kenna, Huddlestone, Konjic, Makin, Tudgay, Bolder, Idiakez, Bisgaard (Taylor), Peschisolido (Junior), Rasiak.
Other subs: Reich, Mills, Grant.
Attendance: 26,160

2 November 2008 – Championship
Derby County 1 Nottingham Forest 1
Scorer: Villa
Line-up: Bywater, Connolly, Leacock, Nyatanga, Stewart, Teale (Barazite), Green, Addison, Commons, Ellington (Kazmierczak), Hulse (Villa).
Other subs: Carroll, Zadkovich.
Attendance: 33,010

23 January 2009 – FA Cup Fourth Round
Derby County 1 Nottingham Forest 1
Scorer: Hulse
Line-up: Bywater, Connolly, Addison, Albrechtsen, Stewart, Barazite (Villa), Green, Savage, Teale (Commons), Hulse, Barnes (Varney).
Other subs: Hanson, Beardsley, Carroll, Nyatanga.
Attendance: 32,035

4 February 2009 – FA Cup Fourth Round Replay
Nottingham Forest 2 Derby County 3
Scorers: Hulse, Green, Commons
Line-up: Bywater, Connolly, Albrechtsen, Nyatanga, McEveley, Barazite, Green, Savage, Teale, Commons, Hulse (Ellington).
Other subs: Todd, Carroll, Pearson, Stewart, Villa, Sterjovski.
Attendance: 29,001

21 February 2009 – Championship
Nottingham Forest 1 Derby County 3
Scorers: Nyatanga, Hulse, Davies (pen)
Line-up: Bywater, Connolly, Nyatanga (Todd), Albrechtsen, McEveley, Barazite (Sterjovski), Green, Savage, Davies, Hulse, (Villa), Commons.
Other subs: Ellington, Carroll.
Attendance: 29,140

28 August 2009 – Championship
Nottingham Forest 3 Derby County 2
Scorers: Morgan (own-goal), Livermore
Line-up: Bywater, Connolly, Buxton (Dickov), Addison, Moxey, Teale, Savage, Commons (Croft), Livermore (Green), Pearson, Hulse.
Other subs: Deeney, Barker, McEveley, Leacock.
Attendance: 28,143

30 January 2010 – Championship
Derby County 1 Nottingham Forest 0
Scorer: Hulse
Line-up: Bywater, Hunt, Buxton, Barker, McEveley, Johnson (Teale), Green, Savage, Pearson, Commons (Anderson), Hulse (Porter).
Other subs: Addison, Deeney, Moxey, Campbell.
Attendance: 32,674